...ment – Significance ... – Mission – Purpo...
...ntribution – Vision ... – Enthusiasm – Wisdom – An...
...Happiness – Joy – Enthusiasm – Dedication – E...
...ss – Congruency – Authenticity – Dedication – Exc...
...ence – Perseverance – Digni... – ...
...Resolution – Investment – S... – Re...
...f – Achievement – Empowerm... – Teamwork – Moment...
...ansformation – Challenge – Teamwork – Inspire
...– Accomplishment – Profits – Principles – Entrepr...
...Cooperation – Productivity – Immersion – Entrepr...
...Scalability – Decisions – Maximize – Leverage –
...urpose – Dreams – Legacy – Results – Rewards
...– Wisdom – Ambition – Assets – Boldness – Da...
...– Dedication – Education – Learning – Growth –
...– Direction – Excellence – Expression – Greatne...
...– Wealth – Passion – Abundance – Determinat...
...ss – Results – Compassion – Confidence – Con...
...rity – Breakthrough – Innovation – Thrive – Tr...
...mentum – Optimization – Maximization – Action – O...
...nspire – Optimization – Organization – C...
...Entrepreneur – Performance – Freedom – Fortu...
...ge – Aspiration – Performance – Autonomy –
...Reputation – Ability – Imagination – Effective...
...Capital – Consistency – Credibility – Dilig...
...Money – Affluence – Influence – Devotion – Alignment –
...pirit – Honesty – Honor – Harmony – Belie...
...– Inspiration – Motivation – Persistence – Destiny – Tra...
...viction – Courage – Experience – Leadership –
...riumph – Mastery – Strategies – Responsibility –
...ability – Scalabilit...

Praise for the Authors

"This is the most powerful, persuasive and practical book on how to turn your business around that you'll ever read. It is full of ideas, wisdom and strategies that will change your business and life forever."

John Gearon, CEO, Executive Life Strategies

"Spike is the rarest of all business strategists and advisors – he has done what he teaches and what he teaches actually works. Spike combines street smarts with business and marketing strategies and the combination is spectacular. He is a true master of business – I should know – he advises me."

Keith J. Cunningham, CFO of Scoreboard and Keys to the Vault

"Darren's marketing principles can make you millions. Apply them, test them and watch the results appear. My business has tripled because of his marketing."

John Gray Ph.D., International Best Selling Author *Men are from Mars Women are from Venus*

"The foundation is the key when it comes to the success of your business. There is no one better than Spike to share with you the building blocks for your financial future. He is a master at laying out step-by-step your road map to success. His teaching style is easy to understand, simple, and puts you in a position to implement for results. When you work with him or hear him teach you will quickly realize why he is so connected to success makers around the world!"

Scott Letourneau, CEO of Nevada Corporate Planners, Inc.

"Darren Stephens helped us in our internet business and within just 3 months we made a massive $2.5 million dollar increase just because of his strategies, so if you really want to be more successful then you need to speak to this guy."

Andrew and Daryl Grant, Authors and Founders of *Our Internet Secrets*

Praise for the Authors

"Spike Humer is a world-class expert on performance enhancement in all areas of business and in life. If you're looking to take your company, your life, or your success to the highest level, you can't afford not to have Spike's advice, support and expertise. It'll be the best investment of your life."

Richard Tan, CEO of Success Resources Group

"Darren Stephens has help us grow our business internationally and as a direct result we are now the world leaders in ebay education and we dominate the world stage, so if you're serious about making money and expanding your business then I highly recommend you speak to Darren."

Matt Clarkson, International Chairman of Bidding Buzz Limited

"Spike's reputation for implementing blockbuster marketing strategies is renowned internationally. He doesn't just get you excited with possibilities, he maps out the method and the exact steps for optimized implementation, and then follows through. In short, tap into Spike's teachings and you'll see your profits and productivity soar."

Chris Newton, CEO of Results Corporation Worldwide Pty Ltd

"In my role, as a business and marketing authority, I meet experts in business from all around the world. I have personally worked with Darren Stephens. He is an inspiring and great leader, and if you're really serious about being successful, listen to what he has to say."

Bob Pritchard, Speaker and Author of "Complex Marketing Made Simple"

"Darren, feedback has been tremendous! Resulting in increased sales... an energetic and exciting presentation."

Russell Palmer, General Sales Manager of Mercedes-Benz

The

10

DAY TURNAROUND

GLOBAL
PUBLISHING
G R O U P

Global Publishing Group
Australia • New Zealand • Singapore • America • London

The

10

DAY TURNAROUND

How To Transform Your Business Virtually Overnight...

SPIKE HUMER & DARREN J STEPHENS

FIRST EDITION (2011)

Copyright© 2011 (Spike Humer and Darren Stephens)

National Library of Australia
Cataloguing-in-Publication entry:

Stephens, Darren, (1964-), Humer, Spike (1958-)

The 10 Day Turnaround: How To Transform Your Business Virtually Overnight / Darren Stephens, Spike Humer.

ISBN: 9781921630002

Success in business.
Business – Planning.
Business.

658.022

Published by Global Publishing Group
PO Box 517 Mt Evelyn, Victoria 3796 Australia
Email info@TheGlobalPublishingGroup.com

For Further information about orders:
Phone: +61 3 9736 1156 or Fax +61 3 8648 6871

I'd like to dedicate this book to my Mom who is the strongest person I have ever known, to my wife Michele who is the sweetest person I have ever met, and finally to my children Kacie, Eric, Alaysia, Steven and Cody. They have been and remain my best teachers of all things important. I love you all.

I'd also like to thank Darren Stephens for his unwavering friendship, belief in me and my contribution to this book and my work, and for his gift of being him. I love you brother.

Spike Humer

I'd like to dedicate this book to my Mum and Dad who always showed me love and believed in me, to my wife Jackie who is the most amazing and beautiful woman I have ever met, your unconditional love and support is priceless, and finally to my children Robert, Michelle, Mark, Bradden, Samantha, Matthew and Michael. You all make me very proud and it's a real gift having such a large family.

I'd also like to thank Spike Humer for his wisdom, strength, integrity and friendship. His contribution to this book has been nothing short of profound and his sheer brilliance lies within every page.

Darren J. Stephens

ACKNOWLEDGEMENTS

While this book is written about creating a plan for transforming your business, we recognize that all businesses are started, owned and operated by people. There is more to a person than just the business side. There is more to you and more to us than just what we do.

Our approach to business is the same as in life, in that there are many facets to success and many factors to achievement.

We'd like to thank the many mentors, models, guides, colleagues and friends who have taught us, supported us and inspired us along the way. Most are giants in their fields, many are geniuses in their own way, and all are gifts in our lives.

In business, people like Richard Branson, Jay Abraham, Chet Holmes, Keith Cunningham, Stephen Covey, Brian Tracy, Matt and Amanda Clarkson, Daryl and Andrew Grant, Loral Langemeier, Marshall Thurber, Bret Thomson, Greg Cassar, Mike Rhodes, Dr. Ian Dover, Richard and Veronica Tan, Bernardo Moya, Koichiro Shimizu, Grant McDuling, Debbie Dragon, Jo Munro, Tony Giannopoulos, Pat Mesiti, Rich Schefren, Brian Johnson, Stephen Pierce and Dr. Tom Hill have been important sources for our success.

In personal growth, people such as Dr. Richard Bandler, John and Kathleen LaValle, Tony Robbins, Jim Rohn, John Overdurf, Julie Silverthorn and Anthony de Mello helped light our path along the way.

In philosophy and spirituality, Dr. Wayne Dwyer, Sri Sai Kaleshwara Swami, the Dalai Lama, Eckhart Tolle, Carlos Castaneda, Marianne Williamson, Ram Dass, Ken Wilber and Miguel Ruiz have served as guides along the path of living and growing.

In health, wellness and relationships, Jackie Tallentyre, Dr. John Gray, Andrew Weil, Dr. Daniel Amen, Dr. Mehmet C. Oz, Robert A. Johnson, Jon Kabat-Zinn and Leo Buscaglia have been important teachers, speakers and authors who have helped us grow.

Most significantly, we'd like to thank Fletcher and Carole Searle, John Gearon, Michael Dean, Luke Raisbeck, Narelle and Jason Urbanowicz, Darren Tagg, Lyndon David, Kevin Stephens, Jeni Stephens, Colin Frankel, Larry Lindt, Mel Kerr, Brian Gerhart, Fred Martin, Paul Dwyer, Manny Goldman, Brendon Bruchard, Debra Kezer, Maria Davis, Vanessa Pedzwater and "Big Bill" McKee for their support, contribution, advice and counsel throughout our lives and careers.

A huge "thank you" to our awesome publisher Global Publishing Group and to the amazing team at Dennis Jones & Associates; Dennis, Joel, Jeff and Janet—thanks for the dedication and commitment to the book's success.

And finally, we thank our students and joint venture platinum partners for their ongoing support and trust in allowing us to guide them to future success.

Table Of Contents

Foreword   7

Introduction – The Night before   21

Chapter 1
Day 1 – Planning For Change   37

Chapter 2
Day 2 – Planning For Change   46

Chapter 3
Day 3 – Leadership and Management   68

Chapter 4
Day 4 – Cutting Off the Past, Creating a New Present   87

Chapter 5
Day 5 – Assessing Where You Are   111

Chapter 6
Day 6 – Planning Key Actions   139

Chapter 7
Day 7 – "Core" Fitness   156

Chapter 8
Day 8 – Making the Right Decisions   168

Chapter 9
Day 9 – Creating Accountability   182

Chapter 10
Day 10 – Creating Instant Wins   206

Conclusion
The Morning After – Sharing Your Findings With Your Team   218

Final Thoughts   238

About the Authors   242

Recommended Resources   246

Foreword

Most businesses are destined to fail. It's a documented fact.

This is a book about how to ensure that your business **isn't one of them.**

The "turnaround artist" is one of the most admired, feared and well-compensated individuals in the business world. That's the person who can analyze a business, make the tough decisions and save the company... or take a thriving company and help it reach new heights.

Many businesses need a turnaround artist to keep them from the brink.

But what if you can't afford to hire one of these individuals?

Or you don't have time?

Better still, what if you could turn your own business around – and do it in just ten days?

That's the premise of this book. In these pages, we will teach you how to perform a turnaround of your business – in just ten days – without interrupting your current responsibilities.

Start your turnaround process on a Friday night, work through the weekend, continue during the evenings of the following week, spend the next weekend completing your turnaround plan, and then you'll put it into action on the following Monday. Over the course of the next week and a half, you will be investing approximately twenty hours on your business turnaround. This will be a concentrated time of study and investigation that will be personally, as well as professionally, invigorating.

Your business will thrive as never before. And you can take those same turnaround skills and apply them to other businesses... for a very handsome fee or even a piece of the action.

Who needs a 10 Day Turnaround?

Businesses on the edge of survival, of course. And if you're in that category in today's economy, you're not alone. Even in strong economies, some businesses struggle due to stiff competition, shifts in the marketplace, or changes in governmental regulation.

But businesses on the brink of a new level of success also benefit from the 10 Day Turnaround. They get to play a bigger game and create bigger results for their stakeholders. Every business can use a tune-up—and some are ready to make that quantum leap towards a higher level.

Turnarounds save businesses. They also create the energy for successful businesses to reach new goals and dreams.

So whether you're on the edge of disaster or on the cusp of massive new success, this book is for you... as long as you're willing to invest two weekends and a week's worth of evenings in your business's future.

Every year, more and more companies go out of business.

Perhaps it's the sheer number of businesses "in business" that makes that number increase. Maybe it's the weak economy. Or could it be something else, like tougher and tougher competition? It just might be the speed of change that every person or business faces on a daily basis. It's probably a combination of these factors!

Perhaps the business started off as a great idea or an entrepreneurial dream, and somewhere along the way the course shifted and what was intended never came to fruition or simply stagnated over time.

The reasons why businesses stall, wilt, wither, or simply don't reach their potential aren't as important as getting them moving again — back on the path of progress and restarted on the road towards growth and profitability. Not every business stands at the pole of an extreme, but a turnaround will serve to nourish enterprises along every grade of the scale.

That's why you are here and why we are here – *to turn around your business and get back to the course you've always intended to take.*

As you read this book, you will be sharing in the wisdom the two of us have gained over our years in business. We have worked with business ventures of every kind, condition and category; the examples and methods we use will help remind that, no matter the desperation of your current status, you are not alone. If you are looking at creating a model to transform your business from simple success to stunning success—we're here to help.

Get ready for the ten days that will change your business... *** forever.***

Yours in Success
Spike and Darren

Introduction

Most people seem to believe that success in business is hard in good times and next to impossible in tough times. Yet if you look around, you'll see that in good times or bad, business gets done and companies thrive.

Believe it or not, you have more control over the future of your business than you might imagine – regardless of the economy, competition, or your own marketplace. You and *you alone* control the destiny, the future, the performance and profit-potential of your business. This isn't to say that every business will always do well, yours or anyone else's. It doesn't mean you aren't, can't or won't be affected by challenges or changes in the future. Far from it.

But it does mean that the decisions you make and the actions you take or don't take have the most significant impact on your survival or success in business.

During times of prosperity and in a surging economy, many companies do incredibly well, some even in spite of themselves. But in an uncertain, fluctuating, or fluid economy like this one, thousands of businesses can fall off the planet virtually overnight.

The companies that survive and thrive in tough times are usually able to do so for a reason — their willingness to adjust and adapt to a changing economy, market or environment. But what does it take to have not just the willingness but *the ability* to change?

The reality is this: *any business that has a solid business plan, strong leadership, and a product or service that delivers value to a hungry market has a pretty darn good chance of success.* Couple that with good marketing, effective selling, clear performance measures, and consistent management and the odds of success increase dramatically. Maybe you have all of these things and maybe you don't.

What makes the difference is knowledge, making sound decisions and taking effective action. You need a good understanding of how your business operates or should be operating. You must know how to structure or restructure your business. You have to develop and implement plans for change and do what's necessary to make money now and turn a profit in spite of it all.

When you sit down and really think about it, business is relatively simple. It involves the straightforward process of exchanging some product or service for something in return – usually money. You give value with one hand and receive value with the other. To succeed, you need to give equal or greater value to the other side and receive more than enough money in return to cover your costs for the value you provide. Simple? Yes, but not always easy.

This basic model is, in essence, all that business is about. In reality, however, we tend to over-complicate matters in business and in our companies. What usually causes the basic model to break down are things like inflexibility, outdated business plans or ineffective leadership. Over-dependence on too few products, services, clients or distribution channels can starve a business when the marketplace or economy shifts.

In addition, outdated information, poor planning or an unwillingness to face a new reality can kill an enterprise. Businesses are often choked by obsolete assumptions, indecisiveness, poor discipline and unfocused activity or the failure to apply their resources in the most effective way.

But a lack of effective knowledge, indecision and inaction could well be the most common reasons businesses fail. These also happen to be the very things ALL business owners can do something about. More information is available today than ever before. Experts exist on almost every topic, subtopic, and micro-topic or knowledge niche. Resources are more readily available than ever before.

Why, then, don't more business owners simply learn what they need to know and do what they need to do? Why don't they read the advice given by countless thousands of successful and experienced business people the world over? Why don't they implement what they learn and take consistent, effective action?

A client of ours once answered that very question by saying, "I would do what I should if only I could."

With the amount of information and easy access to knowledge, for some people the problem involves a lack of focus, direction or knowing where to start. For others, they simply don't know what they don't know or don't realize there is always an answer for a problem or opportunity. Some remain blissfully ignorant of what they don't know in business and what they should be learning; others pick up a book like this and get moving on a higher path to progress. They get into action and turn around their business as well as their lives. (Congratulations—that's YOU!)

The business owners who do nothing often feel completely overwhelmed and uncertain about what to do next. They wallow in the comfort of doing everything they can based on what they have always done.

If you aren't getting the results you want, sitting back and doing nothing different is the most expensive course of action. If you think education is expensive, consider the cost of ignorance. What are all the missed opportunities costing your business right now? What would your bottom line look like if you knew how to shave just 5% from your cost of sale? Or increase your profit margin by 10%? Or increase your client base by 15%? What would your business look like if you got your clients to buy more often, to buy more, to buy longer or to buy sooner?

Yes, these are the opportunities that await you if you are open to making some changes or doing things differently.

But still, some people still want to do what they have always done. So, consider these questions:

What would happen to your business if you were to lose just three of your best clients in one month? Chances are good that the majority of your revenue (and profits) are being generated by a small percentage of your customer base. What would losing your three best clients today or in the future mean to you and your business?

If you're a retailer, what would happen if Wal-Mart moved in across the street? What would happen if your industry suddenly got affected by a dramatic change in governmental regulation? What would happen if the one method of marketing you're currently using simply stopped working? If your most skilled and competent employee decided to leave and become your competitor, what would it mean for your business and how would you replace them?

Such can be the cost of doing nothing or assuming things will always remain the same.

Now that the threat of an unplanned possibility has just slapped you upside the head, it's time to get back to reality. Sometimes outside factors (relationships, economy and competition) can make business overwhelmingly difficult. It can happen suddenly and without notice—do you have the resources to be prepared?

Conversely, sometimes those same factors work in your favor, and business booms. Do you have a plan of action that helps you deal with increased demand? What if you have a giant influx of orders and nothing in the warehouse or you lack the capacity to increase your service? What if you were immediately able to access all the capital you ever needed or wanted, how would you deploy it? What if through the process of reading this book you realized an incredible breakthrough in thinking and in operating your business – would you have the necessary resources to implement and sustain the changes in growth, size and scope it would require?

Most business people really do get uncomfortable when thinking about their business from a perspective of "what if". For many owners or entrepreneurs, it is the very first time they've thought about their company this way — "what would happen if..." In today's economy, with current competition and with the rate of change we all face, a million "what ifs..." have already arrived.

You've been awakened to a new reality facing your business. Still, there is plenty of hope. A late realization is better than never. You want more for yourself and your business. You deserve more — you work hard, you earned it and success in life and business is for you. Things might not have gone exactly to plan as of late but

– great news! It brought you here to this book as a source to turn your business around.

Why else would you be reading this?

Congratulations on your decision to purchase this book. By taking positive action now, you have begun the rewarding journey of taking control not only of your business but of your life as well.

Read the book. Do the exercises. Take heart and take action. There's not only hope, there's certainty in your commitment and your willingness to turnaround from where you are to in the direction of where you want to be.

And as we mentioned in the foreword, not only troubled businesses embark on a turnaround journey. Sure, many struggling businesses implement the strategies in this book and are able to survive as a result. Successful businesses also make the decision and commitment for one reason or another to reinvigorate their company, their organization, or their business model. We often talk about businesses in the red, but the planning needs of good businesses are just as important – probably even more so. Once a certain level of excellence has been earned, what to do about the dreaded plateau? How to sustain productivity and increase profitability? If you've already achieved a level of success but you want to exceed the limits of your current performance, what would you do, how would you do it, and what would it mean in other areas of your life and business?

It could simply be that, in the eyes of the owner, it is not living up to its true potential. Or maybe the owner wants a clearer picture of where the business is right now... and where it can go. Sometimes a business owner just decides to take advantage of changes in the marketplace or of a new opportunity on completion of the business-building exercise. This book is for you, no matter the reason you decided to pick it up. A new direction and improved results await.

The reasons that a business embarks on a turnaround plan are many and varied. However, it would probably be fair to say that during times of turmoil, hardship, or a tough economy, the vast majority of businesses embarking on a turnaround plan do so to stabilize, or even survive. That is why we look at an extremely short time frame in which to achieve this. It should take you no longer than ten days to come up with a powerfully clear, concise, and actionable plan to transform the business. Yes, that's right – just ten days can be all it takes to turn your business around and set you on the track to greater success!

If you have any doubt about the need to turn around your business today, bear this in mind: sooner or later you and your business will have to change. "Willing change" is better than "forced change". The best time to create a turnaround in either your life or your business is when you can "choose to" and not when you "have to". In order to have any chance of survival today, tomorrow and beyond, a business has to be "capable" of change. In order to succeed, that same business has to be "willing" to change.

It's important the choice to change be framed in a well thought-out plan of action. After all, doing something different doesn't always mean it'll be better; but doing something better than the status quo always involves doing something differently than you've done before or are doing now.

By the time you reach the end of this book, you will have a solid plan in place to turn your business around. You'll have systems and structures for implementing, evaluating, measuring and managing a more agile and responsive organization or business. You'll have a clear vision, focus and strategy for the future of your company and yourself.

What follows in this book should take you no more than 10 days to complete. Not 10 *full* days but ten days of attention, activity and strategic action. We've also included an evening to prepare you to begin your journey at the start of the book and a chapter to jump start you into action at the end of the ten days. *You* need to read one chapter each day and then do all, yes ALL, of the action points assigned on that day. The chapters, exercises, and activities aren't designed to overwhelm you—they are geared toward helping you achieve clarity, focus and certainty about what you want, need, and will do to get your business where you want it to go and be.

By the same token, do not try and race ahead to complete the book faster. You need to give each day and the tasks involved your full attention. Make room in your schedule for reading the book and doing the exercises and activities assigned. You'll need to focus your time, energy and attention at least a couple of hours each day to read, think, plan and implement. In order to be successful with this book and enable it to serve you best, you'll need to allocate the time. You'll get out of this book what you put into it.

How you free up the time is entirely up to you. Some people get up early; some stay up late. Other's work a longer day or simply slate a couple of hours in their working calendar. If you simply can't, won't or choose not to set aside the time necessary to commit to your own success or business "turnaround", it might be time to ask yourself the deeper questions of "why not?" and "how can I?"

You might have to cancel some meetings. You might have to take a week off from TV or set aside a hobby for a week-and-a-half. You might have to explain to your family that you won't be around quite as much or may not be as attentive or accessible for the next ten days. And your golfing buddies or social-circle might have to get along without you for the short-term, but you and they will be better served in the long-term by your new levels of success.

This will be a time of deep concentration, strategic reflection and introspection, and newfound commitment for you and your business. Your turnaround depends on your focus over this time. Don't think of the short-term inconvenience or disruption – think instead of the fantastic rewards that await you and your business as you successfully turn your business around, and accomplish all that in just 10 days.

Now... it's time to get busy!

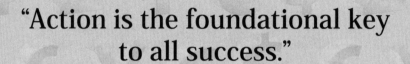

"Action is the foundational key
to all success."

Anthony Robbins
Author, speaker, peak performance expert

The Night Before
– Mastering The 10 Day Mindset

You've finished your work for the week. Have dinner... change into your casual clothes... and head for your home office, den or the neighborhood coffee shop. It's time to kick-start your 10 Day Turnaround.

In order to start your 10 Day Turnaround properly, there is a certain mindset you'll want to master. Having the "right mindset" is vital to successfully implementing the turnaround plan. We want to begin your 10 Day Turnaround on a basis of clarity of intention and an accurate, unbiased assessment of what is and what can or should be.

You have to get clear and be candid with yourself about your business. Clarity is power and it's also the place where new possibilities exist and new probabilities reside.

Let's start with the following five key questions you'll want to ask yourself and objectively answer as you start on Day One:

1. What "is" happening now?
2. What "was" happening before?
3. What "could" be happening?
4. What "should" be happening?
5. What "would" be happening if...?

Take some time and ask yourself each of the above questions. Answer each question in your mind and write a "snapshot" description as completely, but concisely as you can about the key areas, elements, circumstances and conditions of your business. This isn't intended to be a comprehensive diagnostic but a solid assessment of the current reality and future possibilities. Think of this process in terms of creating a one-page assessment and not a wide-ranging prescription or complete cure to what ails your business just yet.

The key here is to develop a baseline of "what is" and to shift your mind from what is and what was to "what will be".

The Turnaround Mindset

Every action begins with a thought or an intention to make something happen.

Effective action begins with effective thinking and focused intent. "right- thinking" creates "right-results."

> "With the right mindset you can do just about anything."

Before you do anything else, it is vitally important that you spend time right now ensuring that your frame of mind is right for what you want to achieve. Without the right mental attitude, an effective focus and clear-headed thinking, your chances of success are marginal at best. With the right mindset, you can do just about anything.

So what is the 'right' mindset? How do you go about changing your thinking or your focus if you're not getting the results you want with your current frame of mind? Interesting question.

Let's start by thinking about what the 'right' mindset actually is. Mindset is a term that refers to a particular mental framework, a pattern of thinking, or a prevailing attitude about what is and what's possible. It involves prejudices, expectations and beliefs and sums up the way your mind is positioned or your thinking is directed at a particular point in time. Whether it is right or wrong, correct or incorrect comes down to deciding how it fits with the task you want to apply it to and if you're getting the results you want.

Is your current way of thinking getting you the results you want in your business? Has your current set of beliefs, biases, and assumptions gotten you all of the rewards and returns you want or deserve? Has your current frame of mind and patterns of perception planted the seeds necessary for your future success? Maybe, maybe not.

For instance, when you are feeling overwhelmed, scattered, confused or simply battered by circumstance, it might not be the right time to make a life-altering decision about your business. Or to be more specific, you shouldn't change your business model, your marketing method, or product or service offering out of sheer desperation or utter uncertainty.

Now this doesn't mean to say that you shouldn't make decisions or implement changes at all. What it does mean is you would be better off shifting your mindset to a point of *focused possibility* rather than overwhelmed impossibility or hopeless improbability. Even in the darkest situations, the focus of the business owner and the organization must be on opportunity rather than problems. Knowing the cause of a problem without defining the opportunity for a solution is virtually worthless.

You need not only hope for something better but gather the confidence that comes from forming a well-thought-out plan of action geared toward the results you want to achieve.

As you begin, it's time now to think a little more deeply about the concepts of forming a turnaround mindset so that you will be able to understand them within the context of change.

The first thing you must wrap your mind around and accept is that "stuff happens". Change occurs – it's a fact of life and a fact of business. What "was" probably isn't what "is", and what "is" won't always be. Just because business was good yesterday doesn't guarantee that tomorrow or even today your business will succeed or even survive. Change is a law of the universe. As Jack Welch, former CEO of GE said, "You've got to learn to eat change for breakfast."

There are immutable laws of the universe, like gravity, that we must live within — like it or not, we're stuck with it. We can ignore gravity or we can be aware of it, abide by it and even overcome it by understanding it. Understanding is the key – it's how we learned to fly in spite of the odds.

Like gravity, change is an immutable law. Nothing can exist, survive, thrive or succeed in its original form forever, but that's great news. Even though life and your business are subject to change, you have something to start with, something to change and something to build on.

All things change eventually. Change is scary for a lot of people. They feel uncertain, out-of-control or helpless. Still, other people feel exhilarated, emboldened or filled with a sense of infinite possibility. What makes the difference?

The difference is the mindset people carry with regard to change.

People who are afraid of change usually feel they are the "victim of change" rather than the "creator of change". One is affected by change; the other is the catalyst and director of change. To some, change happens; to others they plan to make changes happen.

How do YOU view change? How should you view change? How will you view change now, from this moment forward?

You have to have a plan from which to build your foundation; from there you begin to take action. You must have a way to measure your progress against your plan; to monitor your performance and direct your resources toward the right activities that support your plan to ensure the change and successful results. Having a foundation beneath you and the business you are building can go a long way in creating the "right mindset" for a turnaround.

Another fact of change is that success is not always a straight road. In fact, over the long haul, it NEVER is. There will be twists and turns along the way. There'll be bumps and potholes you didn't see or intend. You're going to be faced with the challenge of consistently taking the right action in the face of changes you couldn't predict in the marketplace, your competition, the economy and within your business or organization. You may slow down, stall or breakdown along the way. You must be able to adapt your actions, environment and your approach to keep on your intended course of change and improvement if you want to turn around your business.

The road to turning a business around can be long, it can be hard, and frankly, if it were as simple as having a good attitude and a plan, you wouldn't need this book. If it were as simple as getting started and making a single change — one time — and never having to change again, you'd have made that change long ago and probably be on a never-ending vacation of self-satisfaction.

> **"it's easy to make changes and get immediate results"**

Indeed, old habits die hard. Change is not an event; it's a process. Understanding that is the key to having a "turnaround mindset". Having a plan – one that is well-thought-out and has an intended direction or outcome – is vital. Believing that you can and will do whatever it takes to succeed can make the difference between being "almost there" and being exactly where you want to be.

Here's a seductive proposition – it's easy to make changes and get immediate results and improvement in a business! Almost anyone can do it and I mean anyone; it happens every day.

But it's much harder to sustain those changes.

People assume that once made, a change will sustain itself and maybe even last forever. But patterns of the past re-emerge. People often revert back to old habits, familiar systems and the previous ways of doing business. Old habits really do die hard and there's comfort in the familiarity of the way things were, including ways of thinking and methods of doing.

It takes time and effort to change what has become habitual. And it is less of a challenge doing what has always worked rather than what's needed now. There is a sense of safety in thinking and doing what you've always done and thinking what you've always thought. But when circumstances change, a business that doesn't adjust or adapt is on the road to obsolescence or extinction.

"I don't believe in circumstances. The people who get on in this world are the people who get up and look for the circumstances they want, and, if they can't find them, make them."

George Bernard Shaw

Besides knowing that change is a fact of life and business, what else makes up the right mindset?

Having an effective mindset involves having clarity and confidence in yourself and your thinking. You need to be clear about what's important to you, why it's important, what you're intending to do, how you are going to do it and what doing "it" will mean to you and to others who are affected by your actions. Having clarity and confidence makes it easier to attain the congruency and consistency which are vital to earning the trust of both ourselves and others. You have to find clarity and focus. This is where your Mission, Vision, and Values statements comes into play. It serves as the backbone for growth, providing a standard of strength and integrity. Furthermore, it is a motivator unto itself, reminding you of the purposes behind your every action.

Setting and adopting a turnaround mindset begins with the following four steps:

1. Revisiting your Mission, Vision and Values.
2. Forgetting about the past, focusing on the present, and creating your future.
3. Redefining yourself and realigning your company.
4. Making your mark and focusing on increasing value for your customers, prospects, stakeholders, and yourself.

Your "*mission*" for tonight (and you've already chosen to accept it) is to think through these four points on the next few pages. Invest the time and attention in the questions you and your business deserve and you'll be prepared for your 10 day journey.

Think deeply and passionately about what you want, why you want it, and how you can get it. Consider how you can create more value for others so they have a reason to work with you, do business with you, and choose your company above all others. Consider what your business means, what it stands for, and what you stand for.

Revisiting your Mission, Vision and Values

The following is one of the most important keys to the turnaround's success. Give yourself all the time, space and creativity you need. Take it seriously—take your business seriously—and remind yourself of the meaning of success. Remember that this is real business and that the turnaround will require real work. Whether your business is based on relationships or merely transactions, this is the work that will determine your level of success.
Before you begin the journey of transforming your business, the first thing you have to do is simply read through your *existing* Mission, Vision and Values statements.

That is, if you have them.

Don't have them written down? Don't worry; you'd be surprised at how many businesses don't have a written mission statement. A mission statement is a clearly articulated vision or a defining set of values for a business. If you fall into the category of businesses that don't have a mission statement, it's okay. By the end of this first evening you will have it written down and have a clearer understanding of why your business exists, where you want it to go and how you want it to operate – and why.

If you already have your Mission, Vision, and Values clearly stated — congratulations! But it's still the time to revisit your purpose for being in business, where you want to go and the guiding principles under which you lead and manage your business.

Either way, you will begin the process of transforming your business, regaining control of your future, and embracing the journey towards a more profitable, productive and rewarding future.

Equally important, you'll be clear on what you're aiming to do, why you want to do it and what it will look like along the way.

This exercise will make your leadership more effective, your decisions more congruent and give your actions more impact. What could be more important right now?

So, let's consider what exactly your Mission, Vision and Value statements should contain.

If you already have them for your business, now is the time to get them out and to review them. How well thought out are they? Are they easy to understand? Do they give you a very clear focus of what your company is all about? Are they clear and concise or confusing and full of buzzwords or abstract terms? Are they still relevant to your business today or has your business changed so much since they were written that they are no longer valid?

Your Mission Statement should describe the purpose of the business and its reason for existence. It should focus on the primary intention, the beneficiaries and the value created for all.

Your Vision Statement should describe the business you are building and in what time frame you envision it being completed (in a few well-constructed sentences). A great vision is both compelling and propelling, meaning that it both pulls and pushes people toward something greater than themselves.

Your Values Statement should be a list of what your business stands for. It should clearly express the principles that are non-negotiable as far as you are concerned, so that anyone thinking of joining or doing business with you will know exactly what is expected of them and how they will be treated by you or your business. It should also contain the core values and principles upon which your business operates, what's most important, and the reasons "why". Your business values should be congruent with your personal values and your professional principles. Who you are becomes evident and is reflected in the business plan you create. Personal beliefs and morals will provide energy and sustenance for your business when all else fails. In this way, your personal, organizational and business values must be aligned within your values statement for your business. Be honest with yourself as you evaluate your existing Mission, Vision and Values. What you *do* must be congruent with what you *believe*. When you think about or read your Mission, Vision, and Values statement does it represent what your business is, who you are and what you aspire for your business to be and become? Do you feel a deep sense of connection, passion and motivation when you think about them?

Here are a couple of examples for you to read and consider in crafting your own. Keep in mind, the goal is not to imitate or even emulate anyone else's Mission, Vision or Values. The sample statements below are just a guide for form, structure and to serve as food-for-thought.

Vision statement

EXAMPLE

"McDonald's vision is to be the world's best quick service restaurant experience. Being the best means providing outstanding quality, service, cleanliness, and value, so that we make every customer in every restaurant smile."

Google Mission Statement

EXAMPLE

"To make the world's information universally accessible and useful"

Mission Statement (from a small builder)

EXAMPLE

To be the preeminent provider of superior construction services by consistently improving the quality of our product; to add value for clients through innovation, foresight, integrity, and aggressive performance; and to serve with character and purpose.

EXAMPLE

Coca-Cola

Mission, Vision & Values

The world is changing all around us. To continue to thrive as a business over the next ten years and beyond, we must look ahead, understand the trends and forces that will shape our business in the future and move swiftly to prepare for what's to come. We must get ready for tomorrow today. That's what our 2020 Vision is all about. It creates a long-term destination for our business and provides us with a "Roadmap" for winning together with our bottling partners.

Our Mission

Our Roadmap starts with our mission, which is enduring. It declares our purpose as a company and serves as the standard against which we weigh our actions and decisions.

- To refresh the world...
- To inspire moments of optimism and happiness...
- To create value and make a difference.

continued on next page

Our Vision

Our vision serves as the framework for our Roadmap and guides every aspect of our business by describing what we need to accomplish in order to continue achieving sustainable, quality growth.

- **People:** Be a great place to work where people are inspired to be the best they can be.

- **Portfolio:** Bring to the world a portfolio of quality beverage brands that anticipate and satisfy people's desires and needs.

- **Partners:** Nurture a winning network of customers and suppliers, together we create mutual, enduring value.

- **Planet:** Be a responsible citizen that makes a difference by helping build and support sustainable communities.

- **Profit:** Maximize long-term return to shareowners while being mindful of our overall responsibilities.

- **Productivity:** Be a highly effective, lean and fast-moving organization.

Our Winning Culture

Our Winning Culture defines the attitudes and behaviors that will be required of us to make our 2020 Vision a reality.

continued on next page

27

Live Our Values

Our values serve as a compass for our actions and describe how we behave in the world.

- **Leadership:** The courage to shape a better future

- **Collaboration:** Leverage collective genius

- **Integrity:** Be real

- **Accountability:** If it is to be, it's up to me

- **Passion:** Committed in heart and mind

- **Diversity:** As inclusive as our brands

- **Quality:** What we do, we do well

Focus on the Market

- Focus on needs of our consumers, customers and franchise partners

- Get out into the market and listen, observe and learn

- Possess a world view

- Focus on execution in the marketplace every day

continued on next page

- Be insatiably curious

- Work Smart

- Act with urgency

- Remain responsive to change

- Have the courage to change course when needed

- Remain constructively discontent

- Work efficiently

Act Like Owners

- Be accountable for our actions and inactions

- Steward system assets and focus on building value

- Reward our people for taking risks and finding better ways to solve problems

- Learn from our outcomes – what worked and what didn't

Be the Brand

- Inspire creativity, passion, optimism and fun

Our Mission

The Karaco Team is committed to providing innovative solutions dedicated to guiding our clients towards achieving their goals of Wealth Creation, Wealth Preservation and Compliance with Statutory Obligations.

Our Vision & Values

To be a highly respected Team of Professionals renowned for a Proactive and Caring approach to solving client problems.

Karaco Accountants is a highly trained team of motivated professionals providing innovative pro-active value-added services.

We are committed to building strong and enduring relationships with our clients by assisting them to build their business and achieve their personal goals.

Our vision is underpinned by our 4 values:

continued on next page

Professionalism

For us, this means consistently meeting our profession's standards, continually updating our technical knowledge, identifying professional business partners and embracing new ideas and technologies to deliver innovative business solutions to our clients.

For our clients, this means that you can expect to always receive a dedicated, courteous, complete and high-quality professional service designed to add value to your business and personal goals.

Personal and Professional Ethics

For us, this means that we will conduct ourselves with honesty and integrity and we will be accountable for our prompt and professional performance.

For our clients, this means you will have confidence in our service provision. You will have peace of mind in the knowledge that we keep confidential your business affairs and at all times act in your best interests and within legal and statutory requirements.

Personal Values

For us, this means that we will treat both our clients and each other with fairness, courtesy, dignity and respect

For our clients, this means that you can expect us to be personable, accommodating, attentive, responsive and diligent in all our personal and professional dealings with you.

continued on next page

EXAMPLE

Office Environment and Culture

For us, this means a culture of professional development and personal support fostered by a stimulating, progressive and enjoyable work environment.

For our clients, this means an open and relaxed professional environment with ready access to contemporary and practical facilities and technology.

We have added additional examples on our website if you need more guidance. Please visit www.The10DayTurnaround.com/resources.

These examples serve as a way to guide you in concisely articulating your mission, vision and values, and are not for you to blindly adopt or follow. You should not only craft your own mission, vision and values statements, but they should be written in a way that inspires you, guides you and helps you turn your business into what you want from this day forward.

Interesting exercise, isn't it? If you are like many, you are probably a little surprised, even shocked right now by how much has changed in actuality since you originally planned your business identity. That's okay, because we will be fixing that shortly.

This brings us to the end of the "night before" your 10 Day Turnaround. Tomorrow begins your first full day of work. Congratulations for taking these first important steps towards the re-engineering of your business and getting into the right mindset. You're on your way to recapturing the potential and maximizing the performance of your business. More success awaits!

Reflect on your achievement and celebrate your accomplishment. This day will be a defining moment in your life and your business.

What follows from here in this book will take you ten days to complete. Continue to read one chapter each day and complete all—yes I mean all—of the questions and homework in each chapter on the day that you read it.

It will not be enough just to read this book with good intentions. You need to have your pen and paper at the ready and harness all your energy and the other resources you will need to address the questions that each chapter will raise for your business. You must dedicate the next 10 days to the turnaround of your business. The rewards you stand to reap will repay your efforts countless times over. So rest well, Day 1 is a powerful stepping stone on your path to progress.

"The only thing we know about the future is that it is going to be different."

Peter Drucker

Chapter 1

Day 1

The **10** DAY TURNAROUND

Planning For Change

Chapter 1
Planning For Change

Right now, take out a clean sheet of paper and either write or revise your Mission, Vision, and Value statements. As you see, they don't have to be long, and you don't have to be William Shakespeare or John Grisham to craft them. Just a few sentences on each topic; you can expand upon each area later. As Crosby, Stills, and Nash sang, "You... who are on the road... must have a code that you can live by." That's what you're drafting here. A code to live by on the road to success and significance.

By the time you finish your work on Day 1, you will end up with a mission to live for, a vision to work for and values to fight for. In short, you will end up with what matters most for you and your business.

Redefine Yourself and Realign Your Company

Now it's time to get active. It's time to actually take steps that will lead right into the turnaround process.

The first thing you need to do – and you need to do it right now – is articulate your Mission. It may be that you want to draw up a brand new Mission Statement. On the other hand, you may be inspired by and committed to your existing Mission Statement. Still, you may also want to refine your existing Mission Statement to take into account new factors or conditions that exist today that were not present when you started or thought deeply about the plan for your business.

Bear in mind that what you decide upon here is actually the beginning of your new business plan, so give it careful thought. These first few exercises will affect the rest of your business plan and with it the structure of your turnaround process and the results you achieve.

At this point, it's important to emphasize the importance of writing down your thoughts and filling in each section of this book as you move along. It is not good enough to simply think about it and form the statements in your mind. By taking the time to physically write down the required information in each section of this book you will vastly improve your chances of achieving what you plan. By having a visual written record of this information you will be able to revisit it regularly, further increasing your chances of achieving exactly what you set out to accomplish and more.

Write your Mission Statement in the block below:

Mission Statement.
Describe the purpose of the business and its reason for existence; focus on the primary beneficiaries and the value created for all.

_____

_____

_____

_____

_____

Does your Mission Statement reflect the reason(s) you started the business or the reason why you are in business? Does it take into account the market and the people you intend to serve? Is your Mission Statement consistent with who you are and your personal purpose? Does your Mission Statement reflect who and what you aspire to be? What you desire to contribute to the world around you? Does living, breathing, supporting and advancing this mission for your business create the value you want others to receive? Can you embrace this mission over time and use it as a guiding principle and document for your business, yourself, and your organization? Does pursuing this mission get you up and out of bed in the morning with a burning desire to see it through? If not, keep working on your Mission Statement until it reflects not only what you want to do, but what you want your business to "be".

When you're working to turn around your business, the most "actionable" *concept* we will be working with is your vision for your business.

Vision is the ability to articulate and clearly see what's possible. It's a critical component of leadership, and will help you avoid the "drift effect", which is the temptation to veer from course and head off in another direction. If you know where you want to go and what you want, any time you get off course you'll have a focal point to temper you back on track.

Your vision is the key to creating effective change. Basic change is easy, and anyone can do it. *Effective* change is the cornerstone of lasting success. You must have something to focus on, measure your change against, and guide the direction of your business activities and results — that's your vision.

When it comes time to make a major decision about your business, your organization, or your strategy, you must ask yourself this question: "If we do this, does it get us closer or lead us further away from our vision and where we aspire to go and grow?"

In both your mission statement and your vision statement, you must target your mindset on creating greater value, benefit and contribution. That value is not just about creating merit in your marketplace. It must benefit everyone that you come in contact with or network with – everyone in the world that you deal with. The more value you create, the more valued and valuable your business, products, and services will become. The more value you can create and deliver, the more secure your future will be.

How do you do that? First, understand that your obligation for contribution extends to your clients, prospects and marketplace. But your contribution and value should also extend to your employees, partners, stakeholders, shareholders, vendors and other people who are vital to your business success.

Consider what your value proposition means for each of those people that you deal with. If you can take what you're trying to do with your mission and vision and create greater value and benefit for everyone you serve and depend on, it elevates your performance, intent, effect and results to a much higher level. Having a higher meaning creates greater value, greater profitability, and greater meaning.

With that philosophy and perspective, you will distinguish yourself and your business from your competition. You will have "partners" in your business dealings because your success brings value and success to them as well. Your mission and vision will come to life and be carried by many.

With a clear vision and tangible contribution, you'll create enough value for enough people in enough ways that you'll be elevated to a status and stature that virtually eliminates your traditionally-minded competition.

Most businesses are internally-focused and often ego-driven. When your business is externally-focused and contribution-driven not only does it propel you and your business forward, it also compels people to embrace the same vision for *their* benefit.

Now it's time to get clear on your Vision Statement. Once again, you may keep your existing vision if it is still relevant, but it requires revisiting, and chances are it will need significant reworking based on where you are today versus where you started your business when you first created your initial vision. If your current vision statement doesn't reflect where you want to go or describe at least the direction you want to go, it needs revamping.

In creating your Vision Statement, it's important to remember you should be motivated by your long-term vision but directed by your immediate priorities to **make it a reality today**.

Know this – the future creates the present by motivating people today for what they can have, be, and do in the future as it is envisioned. So construct your vision carefully and wisely. It's not what "*is*" that motivates people or a business to change or improve, it's "what can be". Your Vision Statement must be exciting, filled with the hope of reward for you and everyone you lead or hope to influence.

As you pursue your vision to make it a reality, you will be leveraging the talent, time and energy of other people by engaging them in your vision. Your vision must be compelling to them. People can and will embrace your vision but they will only do so for their own reasons — the hope of fulfilling their personal vision through yours.

Write your Vision Statement in the block below:

Vision.
Describe the business you want to build and in what time frame (in a few well-constructed sentences).

_____

_____

_____

_____

_____

_____

_____

Once again, it is absolutely vital to keep this in mind - a great vision is both compelling and propelling, meaning that it both pulls people from where they are and pushes them toward something greater. Does your vision inspire you? Will it motivate and excite others to embrace your vision of the future? As the present moves into the future, will others clearly see, feel and experience the value of your vision coming to pass?

Does your vision create value as it unfolds — short-term and long-term — for you and for others? How? When? Where? For whom? Does your vision allow others to see their hopes, dreams, and desires coming to pass by aligning their efforts, actions, and decisions with yours?

Now it's time to think about writing down your Values Statement. These are the non-negotiable values you deem absolutely essential for your business as you know it to exist. They are the values that anyone working in the business must understand, align with, and embrace. Once again, give this careful thought because it is going to help determine the culture of your new company once it has been turned around. Your Values Statement will be the guiding principles about how you do business, whom you hire and do business with, and how you guide, lead and manage. This document will be the foundation from which you grow and operate.

Think about what's important to you in life, in business, and in creating an organization. What skills, behaviors, and attitudes do you respect or expect others to have? What principles or philosophies do you admire or embrace? What boundaries or unbendable rules do you have about how you do business or expect others to adhere to? What levels of commitment, performance, or activities do you expect from others in doing business with you or for you? What things are you willing to sacrifice or protect at all costs?

Values Statement.

Make a list of the most important values your business stands by, embrace and hope to embody.

_____

_____

_____

_____

_____

_____

_____

_____

_____

_____

_____

_____

_____

_____

_____

_____

_____

_____

_____

_____

_____

Gut check time. Look back over what you have just written. Does the ideal reality that you envisioned in your Mission, Vision, and Values reflect your current situation?

Hmmmm...

Maybe, but then again, probably not, but that's why we're starting here!

Let go of the past, focus on the present, and create your future!

In the turnaround situation, it is important to understand that the past is the past. Let it remain there. You see, whatever happened back there is history now; it is water under the bridge. It doesn't mean you have to ignore the lessons learned or the underlying causes that created a previous problem, we simply mean move forward from here.

As you affect a turnaround in your business or in anyone else's, it is no use worrying about the past or what happened in the past. You cannot reformulate the past, but you can reorganize for the future. Your attention has to be fixed on the present. Through following the actions outlined in this book, you will be able to mend your problems by developing a plan and taking effective action. If it can't be fixed, then no amount of worrying will help. You'll work around it, minimize it or eliminate the impact by implementing a new model of action. Either way, you'll have the lessons of the past to help you forge a new and more productive future.

Forget the past and get focused on the here and now. We're moving on to the next phase of your turnaround.

DAY 1: Action Checklist

Simply reading through this book will not be enough, You will need to take action and implement the tasks presented for you. At the end of each day, go through the checklist to make sure you've completed the tasks required before beginning the next day.

Consider the checklists your homework and the steps on your path to pregress in your "turnaround".

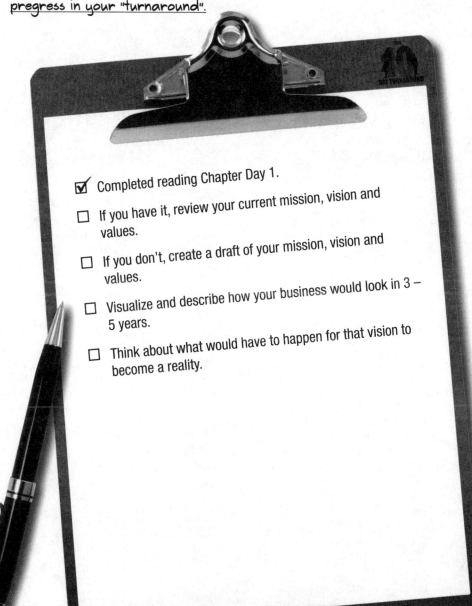

☑ Completed reading Chapter Day 1.

☐ If you have it, review your current mission, vision and values.

☐ If you don't, create a draft of your mission, vision and values.

☐ Visualize and describe how your business would look in 3 – 5 years.

☐ Think about what would have to happen for that vision to become a reality.

"The greater danger for most of us is not that our aim is too high and we miss it, but that it is too low and we reach it."

Michelangelo
Renaissance sculptor and painter

Chapter 2

Day 2

The 10 DAY TURNAROUND

Planning For Change

Chapter 2
Planning For Change

Now that you have revisited your Mission, Vision and Values and done a whole lot of soul searching, it's time to get down to the business of your business. Today we'll build the momentum that will ultimately turn your business around. There's a lot to do today, as we're laying the foundation for everything that's to come in the following days. So let's get to it.

Creating a Plan for Change

Right now you probably have all sorts of pressures demanding your immediate attention. This is particularly the case with businesses in need of a turnaround. But before you give in to the temptation of dropping everything to put out bush fires, it is important to realize that your needs and obligations are what push you away from where you are, but it's your mission, vision, and desires that pull toward where you want to be.

The important thing for you to achieve today is to start generating your plan for change. Without a plan, nothing is going to change — at least not in the way you intend it. You will keep on achieving the same results you have always achieved if you continue doing what you have always done and, right now, chances are you are not satisfied with those results. Right? Let's focus on creating the way forward.

Now if you are getting marginal or poor results (or just results that are not the ones you want to achieve), then you are probably questioning some of your decisions or perhaps even yourself as a business leader. We all have at one time or another. Hindsight has a cruel way of humbling us all.

Hindsight can lead to excessive questioning of our actions, our decisions, and sometimes our own abilities. Before you know it, second-guesses manifest as a lack of self-confidence, including regret, blame, and self-condemnation. You can't afford to wallow in depression.

Anticipation, preparation and consideration create confidence, competence and credibility in business, in relationships, and in life. The foundations to achievement in business are built upon the bedrock of solid and sound planning.

What you should be aiming to achieve right now is the creation of a plan for change. Not a business plan for your newly engineered or invigorated business, but a plan to change from the business you currently have to one that weathers the storm of any economy, market or competition.

Taking Stock

Before you dive in and begin creating a plan to turn your business around, you need to have an accurate understanding of the present condition of your business and the current reality you face. You need to know what needs to change and why it needs to change. You need to know the reasons for change — what will happen if you do and what will happen if you don't go through with changing your business. But that's not all. You also need to have a very clear understanding of what won't happen if you do change the business, and what won't happen if you don't.

This might seem a little confusing at first, but our aim is to guide you in looking at your current situation and the myriad of possibilities you can create on your journey to a better future and more profitable business.

Let's forget about the "how" of making a change in your business for a moment and let's concentrate solely on why you should make the decision to change something in the first place:

1. What do you need to change in your business?
2. Why do you need to make these changes?
3. What will happen if you make these changes?
4. What will happen if you don't make these changes?
5. What won't happen if you make these changes?
6. What won't happen if you don't make these changes?

What you are doing in considering these very interesting and thought-provoking scenarios is looking at your business from every angle. This is important because in reality, most business leaders seem to approach their business with blinders on. They only see what's directly in front of them, what they want to see, or what they are conditioned to see.

We're all conditioned by habits, patterns of the past, and by our assumptions as to what was, what is and what could be.

Question your beliefs and assumptions about what's possible for you and your business. Question your beliefs and assumptions about your product, your services, your customers and your market. Evaluate everything with 'new eyes' and a fresh perspective. Don't set limits on what's possible in the future simply because of what occurred in the past or is happening now. Free yourself and your thinking by imagining for just a moment – *what could be*?

Imagining what could be is the first step in creating what will be in life or in business. Take the time now to get some paper and write down your thoughts and answers to the above questions. Remember, when you write things down, you increase your chances of success.

What is change?

Let's now look at the concept of change and what it means for your business. Change isn't a one-time occurrence. Change happens all the time; it's simply a question of whether the change is planned, recognized and managed or if it is an unintended fluctuation in your business or business environment.

As we discussed in the last chapter, there are two types of change – forced change and planned change. The difference between these two options is huge. Are you driving change or is it driving you? If it is driving you, then the destination will not be one of your choosing, and probably not the one you wanted.

Change can be something that happens or something you create. If you are driving it, it certainly doesn't have to only occur as a result of something negative in your business like when things are falling apart or you are at a point of desperation. Desperation can be a great motivator for change but so can the inspiration that something more is possible.

There are many examples of very successful companies that instituted change when they were doing well and everything was going fine. In fact, some of the greatest innovations have come from changing something when everything was operating smoothly. Think about changes in transportation, technology, distribution, fashion, communications, fitness, entertainment. Often the greatest innovations came simply through the thought that something could be better rather than settling for something that already worked just fine.

Peter Drucker, the legendary management guru, professed a concept of "Planned Abandonment". Drucker stated, "We must practice 'planned abandonment' and give up programs that may work today but will have little relevance in the future."

Effective change needs to be planned, directed, implemented, managed and adjusted. Michael Gerber, creator of the E-Myth concept, came up with a concept years ago that became an adage – work ON your business, not just IN your business. It means you can't just be doing, you also have to be planning, creating, leading, and directing your business beyond the basic function of making a product or delivering a service. Working ON your business means planning and creating effective change, not just when you're forced to do something different.

The reality is that sometimes it's more comfortable for you to keep your business as it currently is, even if it's in the wrong place or facing the wrong direction. Heck, you might even be very efficient at doing what you're doing, even if it is not effectively taking you where you want to go or getting you the results you want and deserve.

Change isn't always easy. In fact, it can be downright scary. It involves doing things differently and stopping some things that are comfortable in their familiarity. Doing the same things, the same way, with the same people can often lull us into a false sense of security. Changing means leaving some things behind, developing new patterns of thinking and new ways of doing things, and creating new habits. Change means risk and sometimes risk leads to failure. But doing things the same way in spite of the results we are achieving or the challenges we face can be the road to ruin. Doing nothing and changing nothing is as risky as life can get.

You have to understand that change is the only path to progress. This is because the world is constantly changing and so is your marketplace. You have to change too or you will become sidelined and left behind.

Innovation and optimization share something in common – change. If you don't change, the best you can hope for is staying the same. And this, as we all know (or should know) is tantamount to a death sentence; the only uncertainty is how long your business will last before it becomes obsolete. But bear this in mind: thoughtful change always beats thoughtless familiarity.

Creating Your Plan for Change

An effective plan for change requires a vision of what's possible, a path to progress and motivating reasons to take that path, clear measurements of progress, flexible action and well-reasoned adjustments when necessary.

Your job in creating this plan for change is to devise a plan suitable for your business and to manage the implementation and monitoring process. Taken logically and one step at a time, you will discover that it is easier than you may have at first envisaged.

Now, it is time to get the pen and paper out again because you are going to need it to write down your answers to the many questions that follow in this chapter.

You have to begin with a clear assessment of your current business and your current situation:

1. **What in your business is working well?**

_____

_____

_____

_____

_____

_____

_____

_____

2. **What in your business needs immediate improvement?**

_____

_____

_____

_____

_____

_____

_____

_____

3.   What changes do you foresee in your marketplace this year, next year and in the years to come?

_____

_____

_____

_____

_____

_____

_____

_____

4.   What one thing could you change right now that would have the biggest, most immediate impact on your business?

_____

_____

_____

_____

_____

_____

_____

5.   What else could you change that would have either an immediate and/or lasting positive effect on your business?

_____

_____

_____

_____

_____

_____

_____

6. What things in your business must you change now and in the near future that will insure your success or stave off decline or catastrophe in your business?

_____

_____

_____

_____

_____

_____

_____

7. What are the greatest challenges both internally and externally that you face in your business?

_____

_____

_____

_____

_____

_____

8. What are the greatest opportunities both internally and externally that you have before you in your business?

_____

_____

_____

_____

_____

_____

_____

9. What changes must you make in your business or your business model that will allow you to overcome your greatest future challenges or maximize your most significant opportunities in the future?

_____
_____
_____
_____
_____
_____
_____
_____
_____

10. In an ideal state, what would your business look like if you were designing it for maximum performance today and for the future? What would it take to get there?

_____
_____
_____
_____
_____
_____
_____
_____
_____

Once you define the current state of your business and describe the future desired design of your business and activities, you must develop a plan to bridge the gap between what is and what will be.

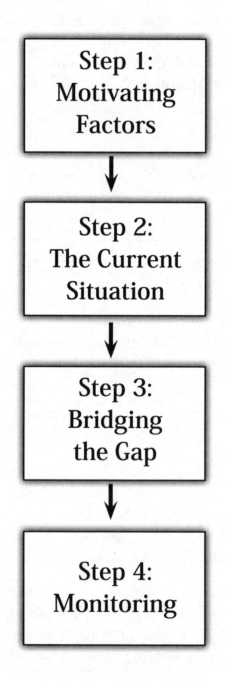

Step 1:
Motivating Factors

1. Write down your vision of what's possible.

_____

_____

_____

_____

_____

2. Outline a rough path to progress – what steps can you take RIGHT NOW to put yourself on the right road? This doesn't have to be a full-blown business plan—just some simple steps you've been meaning to get to or perhaps you're just thinking of right now for the first time. Think of it as CPR for your business... and CPR stands for "Cash in your Pocket... Right Now!" What are those steps?

_____

_____

_____

_____

_____

3. List your motivating reasons to take this path.

_____

_____

_____

_____

Step 2: The Current Situation

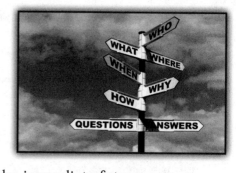

1. Describe the situation, that you would like to change, as you see it today and for the immediate future.

_____

_____

_____

_____

_____

2. Describe how you would like things to be in the future.

_____

_____

_____

_____

_____

_____

3. Why would you like things to be this way in the future – what will you gain and what will you have eliminated?

_____

_____

_____

_____

_____

_____

4. Detail the strengths and weaknesses of the current situation — what is the current situation costing you in terms of money, energy, emotion and other factors; what is the current situation providing you in terms of money, energy, emotion and other factors?

_____

_____

_____

_____

_____

5. How can the weaknesses of the current situation be eliminated, overcome or reduced?

_____

_____

_____

_____

_____

6. How can the strengths of the current situation be expanded, enhanced, leveraged or maintained in the present and the future?

_____

_____

_____

_____

_____

_____

_____

Everything must be up for review and an objective evaluation at this stage. Resist the temptation to do a casual or cursory assessment; your questioning and evaluation has to be comprehensive — no sacred cows, no biased assumptions, no stones unturned. The better you carry out this step, the more effective your turnaround plan will be.

As an example, areas for review, assessment and potential change should include the following, if applicable:

- Business model and strategy

- Organizational structure

- Organization personnel

- Organizational functions

- Job duties and assignments

- Financial measurements, performance, requirements, etc.

- Cost management — expense allocations and cost cutting

- Revenue growth

- Revenue sources and profit-centers

- Marketing and sales

- Product or service offerings

- Pricing strategies

- Distribution models and channels

- Economies of scale

- Joint ventures, strategic alliances, partnerships, acquisitions

- Outsourcing/in-sourcing—personnel, functions, services, product production, service delivery, order fulfillment

- Compensation levels, performance-based pay or incentives, and methods of personnel evaluation

- Benefit structures and packages

- Facilities and equipment

- Vendor management

- Credit and creditors

- Receivables and payables management

- Customer and client analysis and management

- Information systems and management

- Innovation and optimization initiatives and strategies

- Current and future investments and on-going expenditures

Step 3:
Bridging the Gap

1. What gaps exist between current capabilities and resources and those needed to reach the desired future situation?

_____

_____

_____

_____

_____

2. How can you obtain or develop those capabilities and resources to create the desired future situation?

_____

_____

_____

_____

_____

3. What steps are necessary to implement, deploy and direct those resources or capabilities?

_____

_____

_____

_____

_____

4. In what order will you take those steps for implementation or deployment?

_____

_____

_____

_____

_____

5. What is the time frame for the implementation or deployment of each step?

_____

_____

_____

_____

_____

6. Who will be responsible for implementing each step?

_____

_____

_____

_____

_____

7. How will you measure the progress, performance and impact of each step?

_____

_____

_____

_____

_____

8. What are the decision points for evaluation, modification or replacement of each step?

_____

_____

_____

_____

9. What is the immediate and long-term goal of the cumulative impact of the change?

_____

_____

_____

_____

10. What options or alternatives do you have if the change doesn't go according to plan — worse than expected or better than expected?

_____

_____

_____

_____

_____

11. What is the best way to summarize, articulate and communicate the planned change to others — employees, partners, vendors, customers and the marketplace — when necessary?

_____

_____

_____

_____

_____

Step 4: Monitoring

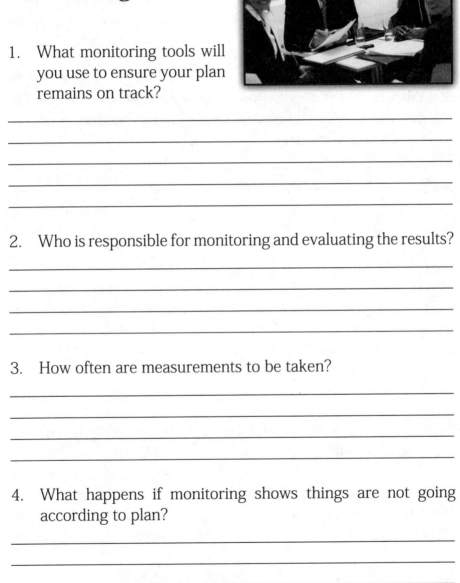

1. What monitoring tools will you use to ensure your plan remains on track?

_____

_____

_____

_____

_____

2. Who is responsible for monitoring and evaluating the results?

_____

_____

_____

_____

3. How often are measurements to be taken?

_____

_____

_____

_____

4. What happens if monitoring shows things are not going according to plan?

_____

_____

_____

_____

5. What happens if monitoring shows things are going according to plan?

_____

_____

_____

_____

6. Who will be the decision-maker or what is the decision-making process to stay the course or course-correct based on the results you've measured, monitored, and achieved to date?

_____

_____

_____

_____

Deep thinking and hard questions are both necessary to this process. Change is a tough master. If you don't ask these questions of yourself and your business, changes in your market, the economy and your competition will still demand the answers. The only remaining question is will you plan and direct your change or will you let circumstance and happenstance makes the changes for you?

Congratulations on completing Day Two. Confronting the current situation and embracing change is not always easy. Remember, change is a fact of life and a condition every business must face and manage. Your willingness to be candid with yourself about "what is" and "what can be" are vital to your current and future success.

DAY 2: Action Checklist

Great job, its really important to get the foundation right when ever your building anything, so tick of the things below on your ACTION check list and keep on going!

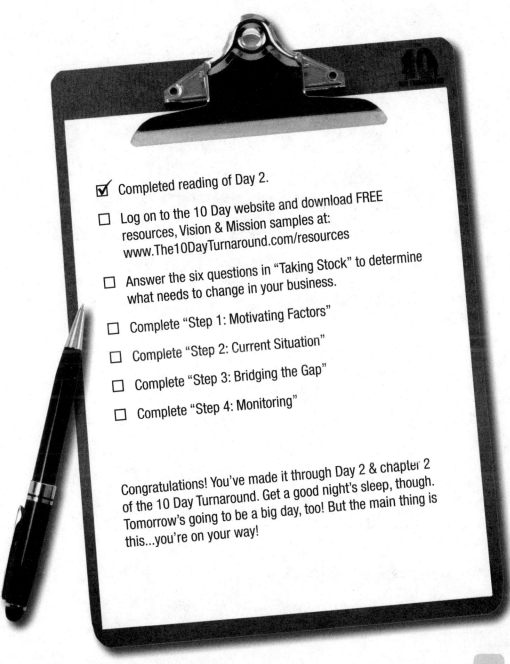

☑ Completed reading of Day 2.

☐ Log on to the 10 Day website and download FREE resources, Vision & Mission samples at: www.The10DayTurnaround.com/resources

☐ Answer the six questions in "Taking Stock" to determine what needs to change in your business.

☐ Complete "Step 1: Motivating Factors"

☐ Complete "Step 2: Current Situation"

☐ Complete "Step 3: Bridging the Gap"

☐ Complete "Step 4: Monitoring"

Congratulations! You've made it through Day 2 & chapter 2 of the 10 Day Turnaround. Get a good night's sleep, though. Tomorrow's going to be a big day, too! But the main thing is this...you're on your way!

"Leadership in a nutshell—clarity, congruency, consistency, and conveying a sense of certainty and inspiring commitment."

Spike Humer
International Bestselling Author & Speaker

Chapter 3

Leadership and Management

Chapter 3
Leadership and Management

Yesterday was a lot, wasn't it? Here's a final note of advice on change: change has to be communicated, understood, supported and, ideally, embraced by all levels and in every area of a business or an organization. If the change can't be accepted, something more fundamental needs to change – either the people or the plan (and sometimes even the leader).

The more committed and effective you are in formulating your answers to the questions from Day 1, the easier it will be to communicate the reasons and rationale for your commitments to change.

Let's continue now, and begin our next session, Day 3 in our 10 Day Turnaround journey, which is all about leadership and management.

"The function of leadership is to produce more leaders, not more followers." Ralph Nader.

Set a Clear Direction and Lead from the Front

To compete in today's global economy every company needs clarity of direction, decisiveness in action, discipline in follow-through, flexibility in adjusting current activities and agility in implementing new approaches. But it's not always easy to move a business or an organization, regardless of the reasons.

You have to face the current reality but you also need to have a vision and an expectation of the new reality that you convey to those around you. You need to have a standard of what you expect of yourself and others. You have to know what you are willing to accept and what you will no longer tolerate from yourself, from others, and from your business.

Competing in tough times, uncertain economies, or simply facing change and new challenges requires strong and candid leadership and a full-out commitment to the cause. Let me give you an example of what I am talking about:

A number of years ago, I was working on a particularly messy turnaround situation, and had called the senior management team together to tell them just how bad things were. I explained that there was no guarantee that we would make it and that I would understand if they left because I wasn't sure how we were going to pay them from that point forward.

Was everyone willing to do what was necessary to turn the company around? Were they willing to do whatever it would take? Before I asked each person to answer, I gave them my word that I was willing to do whatever it took to make the company work.

I asked everyone to search their soul if they, too, were willing to do whatever it would take. (Excluding anything illegal, dangerous or what they felt to be unethical or immoral — ah, the importance of a values statement!).

I asked from everyone right then to look everyone else in the room in the eye and tell them if they were willing to do "whatever it takes."

> **"Whatever it takes."**

Everyone had the option to remain silent, say "no" or simply leave. But to their great credit and commitment, not a single person left.

One by one, they said it out loud...

"Whatever it takes"

"Whatever it takes"

"Whatever it takes"

It became a management mantra. We averted disaster and turned the company around. The lessons learned from this exercise were many.

As painful as it was, people honestly needed to know what we faced. They needed to hear and know I was willing to do everything I could and everything I would ask of them. I had to be vulnerable as a leader if I wanted my colleagues to follow suit.

They also had the right to know the uncertainty of the situation and what they stood to lose. They also had the right to know what they stood to gain if we were successful. I learned a valuable lesson as well – it helps to put commitments into words and to profess them aloud to everyone with a stake in the outcome. When we make this personal vow to ourselves and others to create camaraderie, movement, and motivation, it brings about a sense of unity and commitment not often found when things are assumed or simply implied. Great leadership means candid communication not just delegation.

Looming disaster need not be the only reason for a leader or business owner to seek buy-in or commitment. Sometimes a desire to improve, to shift the business, or to just do something new demands a revalidation of commitment and a redoubling of effort.

You increase your chances of success with a buy-in from those who will be involved or affected in the turnaround process – staff, partners, family members, vendors, creditors and sometimes your clients. This is important because not only will it greatly increase your support and chances of the process being implemented according to plan, it will help keep you accountable and committed to the changes and challenges at hand.

Leadership is vital to implementing change and creating commitment.

So what exactly is leadership? What does this often-misunderstood term mean?

Warren Bennis, widely regarded as a pioneer in modern leadership principles and organizational development studies, has written, "The basis of leadership is the capacity of the leader to change the mindset, the framework of the other person."

That same basis of leadership extends from "the other person" to companies, large and small, to your marketplace, to your social circles or to any other entity, element, or person you want to influence.

Often when I ask an audience for a definition of "leadership", invariably someone will say, "It's the management of others."

Nothing could be further from the truth. If someone believes that management and leadership are interchangeable, I can absolutely assure you they are relying on their title or position rather than their "leadership" to get things done. A position of authority can often get a result simply through forced compliance. Leadership on the other hand can get the same result with less cost, greater reward and longer lasting effect through inspiration and motivation.

Peter Drucker said, "Management is doing things right; leadership is doing the right things." Stephen Covey summed it up this way, "Effective leadership is putting first things first. Effective management is discipline, carrying it out."

Here is one more critical distinction between management and leadership. You manage activities, processes, resources, systems, performance, and results, but you *lead people and organizations*.

If you have to "manage" your people on a minute-to-minute or hourly basis, perhaps you have the wrong people. If you have people in your organization and around you that clearly understand their role, their function, their responsibilities and their limitations, your job is to give them the best opportunity for success. The best opportunity for success means making sure they have a clear direction, objectives, performance objectives, access to resources, and just as importantly the capability of achievement. Asking a first year med student to perform a delicate brain surgery just because it needs to be done and he's willing to try isn't leadership – it's irresponsibility and a liability.

As a leader, sometimes you have to let go and sometimes you have to hold on, but, as a leader, you must always be accountable to those you lead. You must be accountable for your decisions, your actions and your directives. You must be willing to do as much as, if not more than, what you are asking them to do or risk.

As a leader, you have to give the reason why. Why should someone follow you, your direction, your decision and your path to the future? People may not always like or agree with your decisions but they must understand your reasoning and rationale and have the opportunity to decide for themselves if they can support the direction you're going in.

> "As a leader, you must always be accountable to those you lead."

Input into the process of decision-making, risk-taking or change-implementing helps with understanding of "the reason why". If people understand why things have to change, why a decision is being made, or an action taken, it's easier to accept or even support. If they have a "say" in the process it's easier to embrace. If they understand what's happening and why but don't agree with it or can't support it, it's easier for them to leave the process or even the company or for you to let someone go if it's a "hill to die on". Sometimes the direction you're going isn't where people want to go and it's better to find out on the way than have them slow you on the journey as you drag them either silently or loudly kicking or screaming.

Tough times and days of change call for great leadership. As a business owner, you can't escape this charge. Even if you are a sole proprietor, you must lead yourself, your activities, and the functions of your business. This is not only your job; it's your lifeline.

> "Leadership is the ultimate leverage in life and in business."

Leadership during challenging times, such as when you are busy turning around your business, must be from the front. This is because you can't force manageable change within an existing organization — you have to lead it. Effective leaders not only inspire but they also empower other people, an organization or a company to perform at higher levels than they could on their own. This is vital during the turnaround process. If you can lead and inspire those around you to do more than they ever imagined, you'll find success in your organization and within yourself that you never dreamed possible.

An effective leader in a turnaround can't lead from the rear. Get in front, be visible and communicate often and clearly. Let people know what's at stake, what's happening and how they are doing. Make sure the people you're leading know how your vision is unfolding, how much you appreciate them and how vital they are to the cause.

Another great characteristic of leading from the front is to leverage the talent, time and energy of other people by engaging them in your vision — for their reasons, not yours. If you can succeed in doing this, you will have a team that will do virtually anything for you. How powerful is that? Your job as the business owner or leader is to be motivated by the long-term vision of the business and directed by immediate priorities.

Leadership during a turnaround process usually places different demands on the business owner, because many normal operating conditions usually go out the window. This is not the time to form committees to think about "maybe someday we might get something done but we have to develop a consensus after months of investigation, research and contemplation." It's time for action; it is time to be decisive – especially if you want to turn your business around now, not two years from now. As time is of the essence, procrastination has to take a back seat to action. You need to gather the input and ideas from others, but leadership means decisiveness, clear direction, and committed action.

To ensure you fully understand what you are required to do today, here is a short, clear-cut guide to help

> **"Leadership means decisiveness, clear direction, and committed action."**

you set a clear direction for yourself and your team, and lead from the front.

1. What is "*it*" that absolutely needs to be done now?
2. Whose input or support do I need in getting "*it*" done?
3. What are the major steps or activities that need to be executed for "*it*" to get done?
4. Who needs to do "*it*"?
5. How can I set the tone, the example, and be the "lead dog" in getting "*it*" done?
6. How will people around me (internally and externally) be affected by "*it*" getting done or not done?
7. What will they gain by "*it*" happening or not happening?
8. What will they lose by "*it*" happening or not happening?
9. What am I willing to do or not do to make sure "*it*" gets done?

Leadership is the ultimate leverage in life and in business. If you can inspire someone to perform better because of your vision, encouragement or support – that's leadership. If you can excite someone to buy a product or service because of your marketing or sales presentation — that's leadership. If you can persuade someone in a negotiation to see your point of view or accept your position – that's leadership. Without the ability to lead someone in a direction, to make a decision, or to take action, having an effective organization or being successful in business is simply impossible.

> "A leader has to be decisive, responsible, and accountable."

Being the person in charge, being responsible for others, and facing the possibility of making the wrong decision isn't for everyone. It's often stressful and risky being a leader and some people are risk-averse or indecisive. A leader has to be decisive, responsible and accountable for the direction in which they lead, and responsible for where the organization goes. As a leader, your challenge and charge is clear: gather the information necessary to make the best decision possible, get the input from those who can help, obtain the buy-in from those potentially affected by the decision, and make sure action is taken. In times of challenge and change, people need certainty.

As a leader, you have to demonstrate decisiveness, strength, care and understanding— but most of all you have to lead. People around you need it and your success depends on it and on them.

Leaders are meant to lead — they must lead. That's what the word means. A leader is a guiding or directing head of a business or an organization. And they lead from the front. Another way of putting this is they walk the walk and talk the talk. In business it's no different. Great business leaders possess the same qualities and for good reason. Not only are they expected to direct and manage the business, they also have to motivate and encourage the business to meet targets, achieve goals, overcome challenges and push boundaries. They are also responsible for gathering information or input from team members or stakeholders affected by the change process or the decisions they are about to make.

As a leader, you have to see your actions and decisions from the perspective of those affected. A sure sign of a good leader is empathy for others. I'm not talking about "sympathy", although it can be an admirable trait. But empathy is ultimately more effective in leadership than sympathy.

If you're unsure of the difference, consider this scenario. You're walking down the street and you come across someone who fell into a deep hole from which they can't climb out. Just outside of the hole is a rope. Empathy is lowering the rope into the hole and pulling the other person out. Sympathy is climbing into the hole with them and complaining that neither of you can get out.

Empathy gets results because it lets the people around you know you care and you understand the impact of your decisions and actions on their lives as well as your own. Leaders who empower others, team-builders, and inspirational figures gather input and inspire people to follow because of the strength of vision for effective change and an understanding of how it affects others around them.

Businesses take on the personalities of their leaders. If you're indecisive, uncommitted, and inconsistent, so will be your business or your organization. If you're autocratic, demeaning or unappreciative, so will be your staff and employees. If you're upfront, respectful, committed and caring, so will be your team. It's important to understand this because their (and your) very future could depend on it.

It should come as no surprise then that the most effective businesses, especially in times of uncertainty, are informed, agile, flexible and well-led companies. This allows them to adjust to the changing economies, markets, competition and volatilities they find themselves faced with. The same traits are necessary in good times, but in good times it means the difference between being good and great. In tough times, it means the difference, in many cases, between being good and non-existent.

BECOMING A LEADER

Be	**Be** an honest, ethical, respectful, and professional. **Be** authentic, congruent, and consistent when dealing with others.
Know	**Know** the four factors of leadership - follower, leader, communication, and situation. **Know** yourself and what you want to accomplish. **Know** human nature, the people important to you, and what's important to them. **Know** your business and what you do best.
Do	**Do** provide clear, concise, consistent direction. **Do** implement—make stuff happen. **Do** motivate—yourself and others.

FOLLOWING A LEADER

When your employees, team members, partners, colleagues, and clients are deciding if they respect you as a leader, they do not think so much about what you say. Rather, they observe what you do so they can discover who you really are. Their observations tell them if you are consistent in your behavior and congruent with your actions and words. Inconsistency and incongruence leads to mistrust from the people who you are expected to lead, and mistrust can often be taken as a sign someone is one-sided or simply self-serving.

Self-serving leader's employees might ostensibly obey them and may pretend to "follow" them, but the employees or other stakeholders never really embrace a "self-serving" leader or their leadership regardless of their position or power. In fact, quite the opposite; people who work with or for a "leader" they don't respect or embrace might silently oppose the leader through half-hearted efforts or sharing on an "only if you ask me then I'll tell you basis" with vital information.

The basis of good leadership is honorable character and selfless service to your organization. In your employees' eyes and to the people around you, your leadership relates to everything you do that affects the organization's objectives and their well-being.

Respected leaders concentrate on what they are [be] (such as beliefs and character), what they know (such as job, tasks, and human nature), and what they do (such as implementing, motivating and providing direction).

11 PRINCIPLES OF LEADERSHIP

To help you *be*, *know*, and *do*:

1. **Know yourself and seek self-improvement.** This can be accomplished through self-study, formal classes, The DISC Profile (which we'll explain later in the book), reflection, interacting with others and coaching and mentoring. (Know yourself—be yourself, and be truly aligned to your mission, vision, and values).

2. **Be technically and professionally proficient** (do what you do best and delegate the rest).

3. **Seek responsibility and take responsibility for your actions** (own up to your decisions and actions good, bad, or irrelevant to the outcome).

4. **Make sound and timely decisions** (be decisive—assess the situation, gather the necessary information and input to make sound decisions and then DECIDE.

5. **Set the example** *"We must become the change we want to see"* – Mahatma Gandhi (Lead from the front—be the model of what you want others to embody).

6. **Know your people and look out for their well-being** (Know your people, understand their personal mission, vision and values and consider their well-being in your decisions and actions).

7. **Keep people informed** (Keep all of your stakeholders informed as appropriate—your employees, partners, clients, and marketplace.) Let them know where they stand at all times.

8. **Develop a sense of responsibility in your company** (Empower your employees to have a say and a stake in the game they are playing. Let them know how you keep score and how they can win. Help them help you by helping themselves in the process).

9. **Ensure that tasks are understood, supervised and accomplished.** Communication is the key to this responsibility. (Design clearly assigned roles and responsibilities, delegate functions and not tasks, and make sure to communicate clearly, openly and often to convey expectations and review performance).

10. **Train as a team.** Most organizations are not really teams... they are just a group of people doing their jobs, many times in their own ways for their own reasons. (Build a team. In order to build a team it's important to understand a team is simply a collection of individuals united by a common purpose and motivated by their own individual values, dreams, and goals).

11. **Use the full capabilities of your organization** (Utilize resources strategically and align people toward their highest and best use as team members and individuals).

PROCESS OF GREAT LEADERSHIP

There's a common path that many effective leaders follow. While leadership styles often vary, there are characteristics we find that are common to most successful leaders.

- **Challenge the process rather than the person (if something isn't working, it's generally easier to find the cause and fix the problem in the system)** – Identify a process that you believe needs to be improved (it is important to understand the process before suggesting improvements).

- **Inspire a shared vision** – (A vision has to be shared to be understood; it has to be understood before it can be embraced, and it has to be embraced before it can be acted upon.) Share your vision in words that can be understood by your followers.

- **Empower and Enable others to act** — Give them the tools and methods to solve the problem. (Allow people to act upon the vision. Give them the direction, tools, and resources they need to succeed). Give them the freedom to try, fail and succeed within the boundaries of their responsibility.

- **Model the way** – when the process gets tough, get your hands dirty. A boss tells others what to do ... a leader shows that it can be done. (You have to walk the walk, not just talk the talk. If you want people to follow you, give them an example to model and a leader to follow in deeds and action, not just in words).

- **Encourage the heart** – Share the glory with your team's heart, while keeping the pains within your own. (Lead from your heart—be authentic, be honest, and be sincere. Give it to 'em straight—they deserve it and so do you).

Personal leadership is the ability to step up and take initiative. Leading is about acting and inspiring action.

BASIC LEADERSHIP STYLES

		Positives	Negatives
Coercive	"Do what I say"	Can be very effective in a turnaround situation, a natural disaster, or when working with problem employees.	In most situations inhibits the organisation's flexibility and dampens motivation.
Authoritative	"Come with me"	This leader states the overall goal but gives people the freedom to choose their own means of achieving it. Works well when a business is adrift.	It is less effective when the leader is working with a team of experts who are more experienced than they.
Affiliative	"People come first"	Particularly useful for building team harmony or increasing moral.	Its exclusive focus on praise can allow poor performance to go uncorrected. Affiliative leaders rarely offer advice which can leave employees in a quandary.
Democratic	"What do yo think?"	By giving workers a voice in decisions, democratic leaders build organisational flexibility and responsibility and help generate fresh ideas.	Sometimes the price is endless meetings and confused employees who feel leaderless.
Pacesetting	"Do as I say now"	A leader who sets high performance stands and exemplifies them himself has a very positive impact on employees who are self-motivated and highly competent.	Other employers tend to feel overwhelmed by such a leader's demands for excellence and resent his tendency to take over a situation.
Coaching	"Try this"	This style focuses more on personal development than on immediate work-related tasks. It works well when employees are already aware of their weaknesses and what to improve.	It does not work well when employees are resistant to change.

It's time to take a candid look at your leadership style and your leadership ability. Get out that pen and paper again and off you go...

1. How would you describe your leadership style?

2. What are your strengths as a leader?

3. What are your weaknesses?

4. What needs to be said to your team, your colleagues, your partners, or your clients that you've not said at all or not said often enough?

5. What could you say, do, or contribute that would increase the level of commitment or buy-in from those around you?

6. Whose support do you want, need or have that you could enlist to support your leadership and your vision for change? All great leaders require support. It is of utmost importance that you have personal as well as professional people that you can count on.

No one can be all things to all people and all markets at all times. In fast changing times, agility and flexibility depend on having access to whom and what you need, when you need it. Your network of colleagues, peers, joint venture partners and referral generators are critical. Being able to adjust supply and variety of services upward or downward as demand dictates is critical. Being able to access expertise through your network of friends, colleagues, partners, Mastermind group, industry association, and sometimes even competitors is vital since you may not be able to or afford to keep all the knowledge, expertise and resources you need in-house at all times.

Take all the time you need to answer the two sets of questions in this section. You've been given a full day for this exercise, because leadership is such an important factor in any situation, business or otherwise. It's been our experience that a full day is necessary in order to answer these questions fully and from the heart. So please make this the focal point of your day. This is time meant for you to ponder your approach to leadership and to find the humility and courage to improve if improvement is warranted.

It's been a full day! Take a rest, reflect on your answers and your progress and move onto Day 4 tomorrow.

DAY 3: Action Checklist

It's time to recognize and start to bring out the leader inside of you. Leadership is a critical component to success. Leading and managing others and yourself is often the defining element in transforming your business. Understanding your leadership style and assessing your management approach as well as that of others will support you in gaining momentum and sustaining your progress.

☑ Completed Day 3 reading.

☐ Make a list of who will be involved or affected in my turnaround process. (Staff, partners, family members, vendors, creditors, clients, etc).

☐ Describe leadership as it relates to my business.

☐ Describe management as it relates to my business.

☐ Identify leaders and managers within my business.

☐ Answer the nine questions from earlier in the chapter to insure I set myself a clear direction.

☐ Answer the six questions about my leadership style and abilities.

☐ Download FREE Resources from www.The10DayTurnaround.com/resources such as a larger version of the basic leadership styles graphic.

"All you need is the plan, the road map, and the courage to press on to your destination."

Earl Nightingale

Chapter 4

Day 4

Cutting Off The Past,
Creating A New Present

Chapter 4
Cutting Off The Past, Creating A New Present

Day 4

Time to go back to work... perhaps with a renewed vision of where your business, and you, can go. This evening is the time to return to the 10 Day Turnaround. If you're like most business people, you will certainly be thinking about, if not already seeing, your business differently after the first three days of the program.

As your Day 4 session begins, understand that you are competing for today and the future, not the past. Reality check: before you can create what you would like it *to be*, you must confront *what is*. Before you can start healing, you have to stop the bleeding.

Draw a Line in the Sand

By now you are on the path to deciding what you will no longer accept for yourself or your organization. Of course, this has to be balanced with what you *do* want instead. Specifically, on Day 4, we will examine what you are fully committed to putting the full force of your energy, resources, and absolute devotion and dedication towards.

Start by deciding what about your business is non-negotiable. Where is the point beyond which you are simply not prepared to go, to allow happen, or you will no longer tolerate? When is enough, enough? What will you no longer accept from yourself or others? What must you absolutely have, see, do, and create in order to fulfill the image and intention you have for your business from today forward?

> **"What must you absolutely have, see, do, and create?"**

How far and to what lengths are you prepared to go to create the business, the organization, and the success you deserve? What limits and boundaries will you either erase as a limitation or make absolutely certain they become a core of your vision and leadership?

Perhaps your business has reached a level of reasonable profitability, but it's far below what you want or expect. Maybe you have employees, partners, clients, or markets that cause you more grief than the revenues they generate or the cost they absorb.

Is your line in the sand based on no longer tolerating half-hearted commitment from certain team members or partners? Maybe you're no longer willing simply to settle on making a "decent" living versus having the income from your business that you deserve. Perhaps there are certain activities you deal with on a daily basis that thwart your effectiveness or stymie your passion that you are absolutely committed to curtailing or eliminating? Maybe you have certain clients that cause more headaches than profit.

> **"Maybe you have certain clients that cause more headaches than profit. "**

Admit it – there are some things you tolerate in your business that you shouldn't. It's certainly all right to desire more, demand more,

95

and to focus on things that will give you more profit, pleasure, and productivity in your business, if only you made THE decision to draw a line in the sand.

> "Drawing a line in the sand is a commitment, a solid declaration on which you stand."

As business owners, entrepreneurs, leaders and managers, we know there are high impact areas and profit-draining activities in a business that can either be leveraged or eliminated that will have an immediate impact on the performance of the business or organization. It comes down to a matter of making a stand — drawing a line in the sand as to what you do and what you stand for.

Drawing a line in the sand is a commitment, a solid declaration on which you stand about how you and your business will operate from this moment forward. It's a vow to yourself, your team, your clients and to the marketplace that today is a new day and the past is the past.

When you draw that line, you need to know on which side you stand. You must assert what you won't accept, what you are willing to fight for, and what you are going to creatively replace. The clarity of what you are no longer willing to accept must be balanced by the vision of what's possible and what you are intending to become.

Drawing a line in the sand involves knowing your place in the world. It means knowing where you are, where you were, and what's in front of you. Some people draw a line in the sand that will no longer allow others to cross. Some choose to draw a line in the sand behind where they are and vow never to return. In reality — it's both. It's a new beginning. This line—your line—overrides everyone else's expectations and leaves you with the freedom of choice as to what you want to achieve. Drawing this line is a very personal and special act.

We constantly meet, read about, and hear of people who, against all odds, have exploded beyond the limitations of their conditions by making *new decisions* about what to do with their lives. They've become examples of the unlimited power of business owners and entrepreneurs.

How did these amazing individuals do it? They all, at some moment, decided that they'd had enough. They decided they would no longer tolerate anything but the best. They made a real decision to change their lives.

What do we mean by a "real decision"? So many people say things like, "Well, I really should make more money, I should lose some weight. I should do something to get more customers". But if you keep saying I "should" then things won't change!

The only way to change your life and business is to make a real decision. A real decision means you cut off *any other possibility* than the one you've decided to make a reality.

If making decisions is so simple and powerful, why don't more people make them more often? Because they don't know what a real decision is. They think decisions are like a wish list: "I'd like to quit smoking," or "I wish I'd be more organized at the office." Most of us haven't made a decision in so long we've forgotten what it feels like!

When you make a real decision, you draw a line, and it's not in the sand but in cement. This kind of clarity gives you the power to do even more to get the results you've decided to go for, just like this next case study about a young carpenter.

CASE STUDY

A friend of ours, Matt Clarkson, is a multi-millionaire who started his career as a carpenter. After many years of working in the hot sun in harsh conditions (with a bad back due to all the heavy lifting on building sites), he decided to change his life. Matt knew he wanted more, but building was the only thing he knew. Taking any sort of action would take him way out of his comfort zone.

Matt told us about the day he was eating his lunch while on a building site at a millionaire's spectacular waterfront home, when he saw the owner pull in to the private jetty in a luxury cruise ship. That was the day Matt drew a line in the sand.

He said to himself, "I want what he's got. Now I must force myself out of my comfort zone."

The following day he quit his job. Matt bought a lined notebook and went to work scribbling out his most private and important thoughts and dreams. He wrote about his fears and challenges. He matched each one with a plan of solution-based action. He realized it was time to work smarter, not necessarily harder.

CASE STUDY

Matt then created a purpose statement that would act as a mantra for the journey forwards. He wanted to be his own boss, wanted to support a family, wanted to grow his income – and knew all these things required fundamental change. Monday morning, he took his tool belt and sold it. He knew that keeping his tools would make it too easy to go back to what was comfortable and easy.

This way it was a true line in the sand – no going backwards, only forward.

Of course, with no job, no tools, and having a wife to support, he was motivated enough to find something that could create the wealth he truly desired. Within just a few weeks, he discovered the power of selling on eBay. This was a way he could support his wife while he was looking for his new opportunity. As it happened, eBay was "the" opportunity and, within half a year, he was making sales of $50,000 every single month... and it only took two hours a week to run! Now he owns the world's top eBay training system and teaches around the world. Not bad for a builder who went from working sixty plus hours a week for very little to now barely having to work at all.

Matt's line in the sand was the demarcation between an individual who sold his labor by the hour and a commitment to finding a better way... even before he knew what that better way might be.

Once you have drawn your line in the sand, you've got to do something with it. There's no use letting your decision float around in your head. You have to write it down.

But that's not where it ends — you have to act on your decision; you must let your employees, your partners, your clients and your marketplace know about it. You need to communicate what it is that you are absolutely committed to, what's negotiable and non-negotiable. Let your vendors know, your family and your spouse, and your greater support team (your accountant, bank manager, etc) know. It will not only set standards by which they will be interacting with you from there on in, but it will also give them an understanding that you are soul-searched serious about turning around your business. If you want (and you need) their commitment you have to demonstrate your own conviction first.

Believe us, this is a soul-searching, sometimes gut-wrenching exercise. But we promise you the effort is well worth it.

In his dialogue the *Republic*, the ancient Greek philosopher Plato said, "Necessity is the mother of invention". We agree, and reflection and commitment is the father of opportunity.

Problems bring opportunities for solutions. The desire for change creates innovation. Bridges are created because a gap or a gulf exists. Computers were created because of the need to know more and process information more quickly. In fact, your business was created to satisfy a need or a demand in your life, in the lives of your clients, and in your marketplace. If there were no problems, there'd be no need.

If there were no gaps or gulfs to bridge, there'd be no new products, services or a desire for something better.

Celebrate your decision to turn around your business as your moment of truth and transformation; your line in the sand is the beginning of your new path to prosperity and success. It will be your stimulus to take your business to the next level.

Now it's time to spring into action and to commit your line in the sand to paper by filling in the following form:

Line in the Sand

What things am I absolutely committed to creating in my business that don't exist today? What things in my business that already exist do I want to change immediately? What is occurring in my business now that I am no longer willing to accept or tolerate?

_____

_____

_____

_____

_____

_____

_____

_____

_____

_____

_____

Define Your Horizon and Declare Your Commitment

Time to get clear, communicate, act, and implement.

You need to detail and communicate what you are committed to changing so your team, partners and stakeholders in your turnaround can take aim and hit the same target you are shooting for. You need to decide what your business will look like at the end of the ten day turnaround period and you need to take committed action toward creating it.

> **"Time to get clear, communicate, act and implement. "**

Start this process off by first imagining what is possible to achieve. What if there were no limitations, if you had unlimited opportunity (which you do).

We have a philosophy that has been proven throughout hundreds of companies – that possibility exists for all. If something is possible for one, it's possible for all; it simply comes down to choosing the right strategy. If it's possible for "all", it's possible for you. More importantly, if it's possible, you can make it happen. Our goal for you is to turn possibility into probability. It's up to you to make probability a reality and here's where it happens. It's in your present that you can create a new future.

But think about it the other way around for a moment. Is it possible for the future to create the present? Yes. Believe it and here's why: if you have a clear picture in your mind's eye about what your intended future will look like, it's only a matter of working backwards and devising a plan of the steps needed to get you there. Just as when you leave home by car to travel to your favorite vacation or holiday destination, you begin the journey with a clear understanding of where it is you want to go. You then select the map that details the route to get there and you follow it road by road, turn by turn until you arrive.

The other reason you need to go into the future and see yourself already enjoying the lifestyle, the business success, the money and wealth you want is because your unconscious mind can't tell the difference between something that you vividly imagine with intensity or something that has already happened.

Often, when we give seminars, we will say to the audience, *"Would you give a builder/carpenter $1,000,000 to build you your dream home, WITHOUT a set of architectural plans?"* Virtually everyone says, "Of course not, because I don't know what I would end up with", or some say, "No way, are you kidding? If the builder doesn't have a plan there's no way to know if they were building it the way I wanted or that they'd get the job done right".

That's when we'd reply by saying, "Hands up – how many of you in the audience have a clear written plan detailing what your goals are? What type of business do you want? How much money you want to make, who you want as your life partner, where you want to live? How many houses, what type of car do you want to drive? How much money do you want to make this month, this year and in five year's time?"

Out of an audience of several hundred people, we would be lucky if 10 people raise their hands. What's really sad is that most people wouldn't risk spending any money with a builder who didn't have a plan; however they're rolling through life and business doing exactly that. Now we know that you wouldn't be one of these people - would you?

We know from experience that doing a plan for your business and life is one of the most important things you can EVER DO.

It's exactly the same when developing a ten day turnaround plan for your business. There's a formula for change towards excellence in any undertaking that you can use in your turnaround or in your life. A simple, but profound process that will change your world forever; it begins within the imagination of the ideal. Because we're focused on your business, take a few moments to imagine your ideal business.

Ask yourself the following questions to get an image of your ideal business or business model:

- What does "perfection" look like, feel like, and sound like in your business? Write a detailed description of this ideal state.

- Imagine what "it" looks like just before perfection – your life, your team, your bottom line, your surroundings, your state of achievement so far? Write that description as well.

- What's your present "reality?" What does it look like – the here and now? What hurts to recognize? What feels good? Write a detailed description.

Use your imagination. Don't allow yourself to be confined by the limitations of the past or the present; allow yourself to wonder about all of the possibilities before you now in your business. Remember, creation begins in imagination and imagination begins in wonder.

Now create a list with broad steps, achievements, benchmarks, etc., to get started moving from "here" to "just before perfection". What do you need to get started? What do you need to do right now? What do you need to learn or know? What will you need to do, get, create or learn along the way? And what resources will help you on the journey?

Now it's time for you to get more specific, define your turnaround horizon, and to commit to your vision for the ***near-term*** future. These are the actions and changes you are committed to creating starting tomorrow to begin turning your business around.

Remember, the mere act of committing something to paper will give it substance and make it so much more tangible – and therefore achievable. It will also give it life by taking it from the imagined to the concrete. Put it where you will see it every day in a place of constant reminder – your office wall in front of your desk is a great place. If your plan is up and visible, others will see it too. This also makes it difficult to ignore because the mere fact that others know about it is like having another level of accountability.

My Immediate Horizon

This is what _____(name of your business)
will look like on _____(date):

_____

_____

_____

_____

_____

Broad description of the immediate future:

_____

_____

_____

_____

_____

Revenue per month:

_____

_____

_____

_____

_____

Expenses per month:

_____

_____

_____

_____

_____

Profit per month:

_____

_____

_____

_____

_____

What decisions am I making and committing to as of this moment?

_____

_____

_____

_____

What actions will I take, starting tomorrow (or sooner)?

_____

_____

_____

_____

Any declarations or statements of significance in regard to your business:

_____

_____

_____

_____

_____

_____

Now it is time to declare your commitment to seeing it through and doing whatever it takes to achieve your near-term vision. It might not always be easy, but don't settle for easy. Aim for importance and significance but, most importantly, resolve to succeed.

As Abraham Lincoln said, "Always bear in mind that your own resolution to succeed is more important than any other one thing".

Make your commitment to yourself, to your business, and to your turnaround:

My Commitment

I, _____ (*insert name*), do solemnly commit to do **whatever it takes** to achieve the following:

_____

_____

_____

_____

Signed _____ Witnessed _____

(Name) (Name)

Date _____ Date _____

Once you have completed this, your intention needs to be communicated as widely as possible. Gather input where you can and buy-in where you need it. Be open to the "how" but remain committed to the "what". It's your business, your organization, and your turnaround, but enlist all the wisdom, advice, support and commitment you can gather. Never confuse a "turnaround" with staying the same or going backwards.

Hold yourself accountable and ask others to hold you accountable to your desire and intention to change. Profess your commitment and your dedication so you can have more, be more, do more and contribute more. Don't settle and don't allow others to settle for less than you want or deserve with your business.

The more people by whom you are held accountable, the better. People who have the greatest stake in your success are best to first hear your commitment. Since their future and fate is in some way aligned with yours, it's your obligation to share it. Next, tell the people who have the greatest willingness and opportunity to help you, support you, and guide you. Forget about people who love you too much to hurt your feelings or people who simply tell you what you want to hear — they may be comforting but they're not the people to best hold you accountable to your commitment. Tell people you respect, tell people you want to be more like. This message will bond you very well to a great many individuals.

Finally, prepare yourself to share this process or your plans with your entire team or organization. Involve them if you can, and communicate with them if you can't involve them. But let people most important and impacted by your plans, commitments, and declarations know what you intend to do and aspire to be. Let them know that you are serious about "turning the business around", whether it be significant or subtle, their livelihoods are affected by your actions and decisions. If they understand the level of your commitment, they will be more inclined to share their input, ideas, their heart and soul, and fiercely commit to it themselves, giving you even more chance of successfully achieving your goals.

Create a Measurable Strategy

You're committed to change — it's clear in your mind and it should be congruent in your heart. The important thing to remember when designing a turnaround strategy is that to make your intention a reality it needs to be measurable. You need to have some way of gauging whether you, your strategy and your business are producing the desired results or not. At the very least, you want to know whether it is taking your business in the direction you intended.

> **"We lie loudest when we lie to ourselves."**

Ask yourself the tough questions right now. Be honest with yourself. Eric Hoffer said, "We lie loudest when we lie to ourselves."

Now is not the time to get defensive, to rationalize or procrastinate. It's time to do what you say, do it the best way you know how, and do it as fast as you can — without excuse and without retreat.

You know what you want and you know the major decisions you need to make and the most important and immediate actions you need to take, but what else?

There's more to your story than a few immediate decisions and actions.

There's more that you need to do and there are certain things you need to stop doing immediately that will speed your success. You might not have all the answers or details of your strategy but you know there are certain activities that help or hinder your business.

Years ago, I learned a great lesson from our colleague Brian Tracy, the author, entrepreneur and sales master. He taught me a model I use to this day in implementing any major change or shift in my life or business.

Evaluate your current habits, activities, decisions, strategies and tactics. Make a list of the following:

- Things you will start doing
- Things you will stop doing
- Things you will do more of or do more often
- Things you will do less of or do less often

After all, if something is going to change, something has to change – here is where change begins.
Asking yourself the right questions will lead you on the path to finding the right answers and creating the best strategy.

Now that you know what you want to achieve and have an idea of how to get started, ask yourself:

What are the major actions, activities, benchmarks and guideposts that I'll use to measure my progress?

- What are the incremental steps I can take to accomplish my most important goals?
- What is the most important thing I can do right now?
- What information, knowledge, or resources do I need?
- What information, knowledge, or resources do I have available?
- How and where can I access what I need but don't yet have?

Find a mentor; create a Mastermind group, network, or form a peer group of people and business owners who are committed to excellence, turning around their business, or simply passionate about living up to their ultimate potential.

A role model or resource group could be one of your most important assets because when you are turning around your business, you don't have time, money or energy to waste. Others have been where you are now and have come up with solutions, so why not learn from them? Having someone to bounce ideas off, brainstorm with, or share insights and experiences with is one of the best things in life — especially if they are knowledgeable and experienced in business and the challenges you're facing.

You may even like to work with us as your mentors. To find out how, just visit our website at www.The10DayTurnaround.com

Finally, build in a system or a reporting structure to tell you whether you are getting closer or further away from your goals as you implement your turnaround strategy. What information will you need? What are your key indicators of success? Of course you need to measure sales, expenses, cash flow, current cash, assets, obligations and debt. But what else?

Think about things like the number of clients you have, the profit value/contribution of each client, the number of times a client buys, the size of their transaction, and how often and long they buy from you.

What are your clients telling you in their feedback, buying patterns and by their activity or inactivity?

Assess your selling methods and sales conversion ratios. Review your ROI on your marketing activities and on every recurring or episodic expense you have.

During a turnaround you have to look at every dollar you make and every dollar you spend as a step closer or farther away from your vision for change and your commitment to improvement.

> "look at every dollar you make and every dollar you spend "

In one-on-one client work, we emphasize the importance of a Key Performance Indicator Report Card. We work together to create one during this part of the turnaround process.

It's easier to assess your future performance once you know where you are, what it's costing you to stay there, and how much money you're making by being there.

What you have to do here is to come up with a strategy that you are going to use to turbo-charge your business in a very short period of time. You will be sweeping aside everything you have traditionally been doing and forgetting about the way you have been going about it. You see, the one thing you don't want to be doing going forward is continue doing the things the same way you did in the past. Why would you want to when clearly they didn't work, otherwise you wouldn't be in the midst of a turnaround exercise right now, would you?

What is the one thing you need to do to reinvigorate your business? Decide on that and then develop a measurable strategy to put that in place. Prioritize according to your principles. And remember, fortune favors the fast – so get an idea, make a decision and take action. That's all you have to do right now.

Communicate, Communicate, Communicate

> "If your actions inspire others to dream more, learn more, do more and become more, you are a leader."

Leading from the front is all about clear, concise communication. It is also about being decisive and taking action. Leading by example is how it is also often described.

John Quincy Adams said, "If your actions inspire others to dream more, learn more, do more and become more, you are a leader."

Leadership is about setting direction, making decisions, communication and inspiring others to take action on a clear path to improvement.

The point about setting a clear direction for your business is often misunderstood. The operative word here is 'clear'. It must not only be clear in its conception and planning, it must also be clearly understood by your entire team.

It's not enough to keep this knowledge to yourself; it has to be clear in the minds of your entire team and gain the support of anyone who is vital to the new direction.

If you're a business owner with lots of employees, vested partners or public

> **"leaders and entrepreneurs are often visionaries"**

shareholders, often you'll have to articulate your vision to the wider stakeholder community. You'll have to work on convincing this stakeholder community that your new direction is not only viable but in their best interest, not just yours.

Because leaders and entrepreneurs are often visionaries, they sometimes see things that others can't or see them long before others can feel the same sense of possibility.

Most people don't grasp or understand what it takes to be a business owner or entrepreneur; they also seldom see what the leader of a business has to do to bring a vision, a new direction or a turnaround about in an organization.

Leaders not only have to convince stakeholders that they have the right plan, with the right resources, and the skill to make the right decisions along the way, they also need to engage and earn the confidence of the people around them. The only way to achieve this is through communication, and lots of it.

The best business leaders are exceptional communicators; they have to be. You can't expect people to read your mind in good times, let alone in times of uncertainty. Don't assume the people you depend on understand what you understand, know what you know, or think like you think.

George Bernard Shaw said, "The single biggest problem in communication is the illusion that it has taken place."

People who are affected by your leadership, your decisions, and your turnaround actions have a right to know why things are changing. They should know what you know about the challenges and opportunities if they are expected to support your direction and leadership. The only way they can do that is if they hear, see, and feel what you're thinking.

Before you leave Day 4, determine your **turnaround communication plan:**

1. What do I need to communicate?

2. To whom do I need to communicate it?

3. What is the best way to communicate it?

4. How often does it need to be communicated?

5. What is the process for gathering input, ideas, information and support from others along the way?

DAY 4: Action Checklist

The ability to see beyond the present moment and imagining what's possible is vital to your immediate and long term future. This ability backed up by a process of taking measured, strategic action is the catapult to propel you from where you are to where you want to be. Your ability to communicate your vision and your strategy creates leverage, loyalty, and synergy in your resources, people, partners, and stakeholders. We communicate even when we don't speak so now is the time to start to stand up, standout, and start to share your passion, commitment and vision.

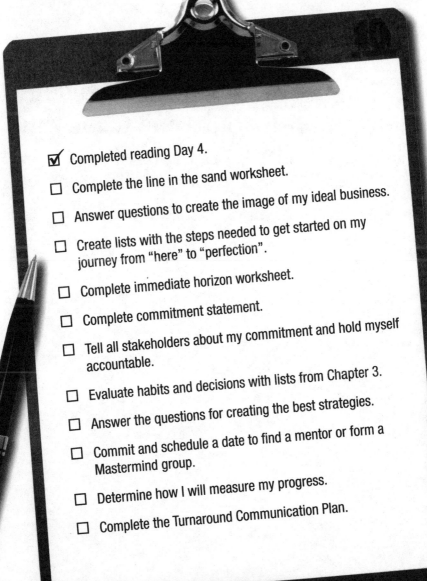

- ☑ Completed reading Day 4.
- ☐ Complete the line in the sand worksheet.
- ☐ Answer questions to create the image of my ideal business.
- ☐ Create lists with the steps needed to get started on my journey from "here" to "perfection".
- ☐ Complete immediate horizon worksheet.
- ☐ Complete commitment statement.
- ☐ Tell all stakeholders about my commitment and hold myself accountable.
- ☐ Evaluate habits and decisions with lists from Chapter 3.
- ☐ Answer the questions for creating the best strategies.
- ☐ Commit and schedule a date to find a mentor or form a Mastermind group.
- ☐ Determine how I will measure my progress.
- ☐ Complete the Turnaround Communication Plan.

"Money gives you the freedom to do with your time what you want to do with it."

Richard Branson
Entrepreneur & Billionaire

Chapter 5

Day 5

Assessing Where You Are

Chapter 5
Assessing Where You Are

Congratulations – after tonight, you'll be halfway done with the 10 Day Turnaround!

We're sure you're tired from a long day of work and perhaps less sleep than usual, because you were working hard last night on Day 4. But if you're serious about the program, you've got to stay with it... and the fact that you're still reading means that you are serious. We applaud you for that! So let's get down to business and start the work of Day 5.

Turning around a business is just like taking a trip – perhaps not a vacation, but a journey just the same. It's a journey of exploration and discovery because you are sure to realize things about yourself and your business that you never knew, perhaps things long forgotten or that you haven't really wanted to face in the past.

Assessing the Present and Aligning the Future

When you think about changing anything, you need to know what is, perhaps what was, and what can be. You also need to know what it will take to go from where you are to where you want to go. It's a significant undertaking but simpler than it may appear at first.

Where are you today? Describe your business as it exists today:

1. Description of the business model
2. Description of the products and services offering
3. Current and projected revenues
4. Current and projected profits
5. Current and projected cash flows
6. Current and projected number of clients or customers
7. Historical and projected number of total sales or transactions
8. Historical and projected number of sales or transactions per client or customer
9. Historical and projected dollar size of sales or transactions per client or customer
10. Historical and projected frequency of sales or transaction per client or customer
11. Current and projected number of employees
12. Describe and record any other relevant or significant facts, information or factors about the present state of your business and projected operations.

Note: While it's important to track, measure, and report your business on an annual basis, for purposes of this exercise, we recommend using monthly, quarterly and annualized numbers/productions.

Obviously, where you are is not where you want to be, think you should be, or where you could be – otherwise, you wouldn't be reading this book. So now it's time to think about your immediate future.

In turnaround planning, horizons are typically shorter than the normal business planning processes. Generally, the more urgency in the need of a "turnaround" the shorter the planning horizon will be for this exercise. To keep your commitment to change tangible and actionable, we recommend using a three to six month time horizon in answering the following questions.

The answers to some of these questions may remain the same as when you answered them moments ago (things like the description of your business model). Other answers may be dramatically different.

1. Description of the desired business model
2. Description of the desired products and services offering
3. Desired revenues at:
    - Three months
    - Six months
4. Desired profits at:
    - Three months
    - Six months
5. Desired cash flows at:
    - Three months
    - Six months
6. Desired number of clients or customers at:
    - Three months
    - Six months

7. Desired number of total sales or transactions at:

   - Three months
   - Six months

8. Desired number of sales or transactions per client or customer at:

   - Three months
   - Six months

9. Desired dollar size of sales or transactions per client or customer at:

   - Three months
   - Six months

10. Desired frequency of sales or transaction per client or customer at:

    - Three months
    - Six months

11. * Desired number of employees at:

    - Three months
    - Six months

12. Describe and record any other relevant or significant facts, information or factors about the desired state of your business and projected operations at:

    - Three months
    - Six months

> * It might be helpful to think about the number of employees per client, transaction, ratio to revenue, or some other variable-based assessment rather than simply a number of employees. Perhaps your plan would include having fewer employees and more independent contractors, strategic alliances, or joint venture partners.

Before we get into the "tactical how" of bridging the gap between the current reality and the desired short-term future, there are a few things we must do.

If you intend to change something – **_anything_** – you should think about it first in these terms:

1. If I get what I want, what will it give me?

_____

_____

_____

_____

_____

2. If I get what I want, what will it cost me?

_____

_____

_____

_____

Pretty simple questions to answer – but not knowing what you will gain or what you stand to lose is a source of many short-lived or failed changes.

We're assuming that if you're an entrepreneur or business owner, you probably want more profit (or at least the same profit) if you're intending to make a change. You'd probably like a bit more time, freedom and less complication in your life. Most business people would love to have the ability to create more value or deliver value to more people. Sometimes our goals, objectives or wishes get misaligned or cause conflict in our lives.

We'll share a client story with you.

A number of years ago, I was hired by a company to grow it dramatically. The challenge was unique in the sense they had all the sales they wanted, in fact, far more than they could fill. Huge money was being left on the table and opportunities for growth were being lost every day.

Believe it or not, the problem was easy to solve. We took a small boutique manufacturing operation and turned it into a highly-tuned manufacturing machine – seven days a week, twenty-four hours a day they were cranking out products *and profit*. Success! (And success in a very short period of time I might add.)

But then, something strange happened. The owner and creative driver of the company had doubts and lost their zeal for the business. They were making more money than ever before. Their clients were ecstatic. They were bringing in new clients and buyers at a rate thought impossible just months before.

What could possibly be wrong with that? It's what they wanted and why they brought me in.

Well, there was a severe disconnect between the new reality and the imagined one. What the owner hadn't envisioned was having to own, operate and be responsible for nearly three times the employees, a client base that had quadrupled, and the complexities of having a business about five times the size.

The owner was passionate about making a good living, having the time and freedom that comes with a small profitable business and not the complexities of having a larger, albeit much more profitable enterprise. The present reality was not making him happy.

So again, I ask as you think about what you want for the future and for your business:

1. If I don't get what I want, what won't it give me?
2. If I don't get what I want, what won't it cost me?

Asking, thinking about, and formulating answers to the right questions is the key to all effective and successful change – in life or business, in organizations, or in individuals.

Don't let the questions throw you. These profoundly different questions will create significantly different perspectives and hopefully vividly distinct answers for your future. If you sense a disconnect between what you want to do and what you think it will give you, cost you, prevent you from having, or not "save" you enough after you answer these questions, pay close attention.

Lasting change needs lasting commitment. If you feel uncertain about the future you're creating in the short-term, you'll never sustain it in the long-term. Your turnaround should not only serve your business, it should serve you, your mission, your vision and your values.

Assuming you feel good in your head, heart and gut about the changes you want to make in the immediate future—it's time to get to the art of making it happen.

> "it's time to get to the art of making it happen."

You might already have a sense of what needs to happen starting today to bridge the gaps toward the next three to six months. These could be sweeping changes, or a tactical tweak here or there that has an immediate impact in getting things done.

We'll begin the process by having you write a "gut-feel", "off-the-top-of-your-head" description of how to get started. This exercise isn't the sweeping, long-term, strategic plan for change you were working on earlier in the book. This is the place for fast impact and quick wins. What needs to be done now? What can be done now? How can it be done now to get from where I am to where I want to be in three months or six months?

I like to start with a one page, perhaps two page at most, description of what has to happen, what's going to happen, who's going to make it happen, and when. When it comes to the "who", I start with what I can do.

You'll always have the most flexibility, adaptability, and control over your own actions so begin with your highest "probability of directability" and commit yourself to action.

It's a way to lead by example and set the pace for the rest of your organization or stakeholders to follow.

If you're looking to hire someone either to be part of your organization or as an outside consultant to help in your turnaround, don't allow yourself or your business to be seduced by complexity, buzzwords, jargon or magic formulas for change in your business that someone else tells you. The best bet is to open your mind as well as your heart and let the answers surface. That is not something another person can be hired to do.

Some consultants, trainers or "hired guns" earn a lot of money making a simple thing appear hard, unapproachable or overly-complex. It makes them seem like deep thinkers! People inside and outside your organization should get paid to make things simple and to get things done — perhaps not pretty, but certainly effective.

Seems pretty basic — almost simplistic or blatantly obvious — but so many entrepreneurs, business owners, managers or executives ignore the obvious. It's almost as if they believe it has to be complicated or come from "without" rather than from "within" to make a change or to create a plan for a "turnaround".

Turning a business around is not a mystical process; anyone who tells you that explicitly or implicitly should be viewed with suspicion at best and "invited" to take their advice down the street.

> **"Aim for simplicity and activities that get impressive results."**

When we go into a business a client expects "results". They don't want to hear about the latest research, trend or management philosophy; they just want improvements made now. Aim for simplicity and activities that get impressive results rather than proposals, resumes and consultants who merely sound impressive.

The information, knowledge and experience you have at your disposal are far greater than any book, consultant, external expert or guru could ever give you. Your own wisdom about your business, organization, products, services, clients, prospects and market should be the source of your plan for progress.

Once you have a rough plan of action, begin to formulate a series of incremental, sequential steps of activity you believe to be the best course of action based on the information you have right now.

Begin creating a list of "to-do's", a series of strategies, and a system of activities to begin your plan for change. They won't all work — guaranteed. But your highly-seasoned experience about your business will serve you well as a start.

> **"Don't pretend that "knowing" what to do is the same as "doing" it."**

Don't look to make things complex. Don't get hung up on the difficulty of "everything" that needs to be done. Just get moving, don't stop moving, and get other people moving as you work out your rough plan of action.

Don't allow yourself to simply think about or "talk" about what needs to be done. Don't pretend that "knowing" what to do is the same as "doing" it.

Get started on your "to-do's" right away. Start where you think you can have the biggest, most immediate impact but get started. Get something "done".

A great friend and brilliant colleague of mine, Dave Bernstein, is fond of saying he doesn't have a "to-do" list, he only has an "it's done" list. What's on his list is considered "done". I strive for the same speed of result and so should you in your turnaround.

After you begin to implement your "rough" plan of action, make sure to observe, measure, and monitor your results. What works, you continue or expand; what doesn't you either stop, decrease or modify.

Once you have a bit of feedback from the results of implementing your rough plan of action, it's time to adjust. Ramp it up if it's working — speed it up, roll it out, wind it down, or phase it out.

If what you're doing is working, then make those same things happen all over again — maybe even faster and broader by engaging others inside and outside of your business to break through your limitation of the past.

I know it seems simple and quite frankly it is, although not necessarily easy. Doing a turnaround in your business isn't the time for "fancy"; it's the time for "effective".

Start by sorting out what works in your plan versus what doesn't work as planned. Scale it up, roll it out, and get people doing what you're doing so you can move on to other things. If you're a solo-operator or a small entrepreneur, do what you do best, what has the highest and most immediate positive impact in your business and either eliminate or outsource the rest.

> **"Ignore those who say your "it" can't be done"**

And remember that you cannot do any of this alone. Listen to those people around you who have a desire for input and clear ideas about how to make things better. Ignore those who say your "it" can't be done or it can't be done so fast without offering other ideas to make improvement happen. Fire those who say either out loud with their words or silently with their actions that they are not part of the plan to turn your business around.

Some words of advice...

Demand of yourself and others to communicate plainly and clearly, especially when you're beginning to communicate your rough plan and the immediate actions that need to be taken.

Take the fuzzy, the complicated and the mysterious and make it obvious. People understand the obvious and when understood the obvious gets done. Look to create systems and structures that anyone can duplicate and sustain beyond your own immediate actions. If you want, need or hope to have someone else do what you can do, are doing, or need to do, you need to make it sustainable and scalable through others, either now or in the future.

Lay out what needs to be done, by whom, when, and what the consequences – good or bad – will be if you're

> **"Lay out what needs to be done."**

making progress or not. A business owner has to push through denial and grasp what can realistically be done right away; and what can get the highest, most immediate impact possible.

Asset Inventory and Liability List

This is part of point one of **"Seven Secrets of Getting Significant Things Done"**. The starting point for developing an asset inventory and liability list is to develop absolute clarity about your current situation. Look at your overall business and ask, "What's working?" and "What's not working?" in every area.

Where are you now? What is your current level of sales? Break them down by product, product line, service, and market and distribution channel. What exactly are you selling? Who are you selling to, at what prices, and what is the level of profitability? What is your market? Who are your clients or customers and why do they do business with you?

Next, compare your current sales with your business plan; what sales assumptions does it contain, what are your expectations and what are your sales projections? Are you on track to achieve them? How did your sales turn out last year? Are there any trends you can see? If so, are they up or down? Is this trend temporary or permanent? Can you deduce anything from these trends? What could you do to respond more effectively to them?

Next look at your cash flow and levels of profitability from each product, service and area of activity. How are they tracking? Up or down? How do they stack up compared to your budget? What about the percentages. Are your return-on-equity, return-on-investment, and return-on-sales figures telling you anything? Do you know how to read and interpret these reports? Do you understand what the figures mean? If not, what should you be doing about this?

You see, what you have to realize here is that, if you are serious about turning your business around in just ten days, you are going to have to ask yourself really hard questions. Don't avoid a question just because you know the answer is going to be painful, difficult, or involve change.

Ask yourself this broad question about every major activity and resource investment you're undertaking and making in your business, "Should we be doing something else or should we do more of what we are already doing?"

Which of your products or services are selling well and which aren't? Which are profitable and which are draining your reserves? What you are ultimately looking to see is whether your business is healthy or not.

I cannot over-emphasize one key point: *clarity is the key*. This means that you have to be absolutely clear about the answers to each of these questions. Anything short of absolute clarity will result in time-wasting, missed opportunities and perhaps even failure.

Don't forget to delve into areas distinct from your product or service line-up. Include in your inventory the most important skills and competencies that your company possesses. Who are your most valuable team members? Who is a liability to the future of your business? Who are your best customers? Who could you not afford to lose and who can you not really afford to keep doing business with? What and where are your best markets? What do your customers like the most about what you do for them? What do they like the least?

Now turn the spotlight on you, the business owner or leader. It is absolutely essential that you remain objective and honest during this process, no matter how painful and revealing this may be. What are you good at doing? What are your best qualities and abilities? What are the most valuable contributions you make to your business? Aim for the facts because facts don't lie. You need to uncover the truth about your situation; otherwise you won't be able to make meaningful change.

How about your assumptions? Take a good hard look at them and ask yourself if they are still relevant. Assumptions that were made in error are at the root of all failures. If you discovered you had based your business model on a set of false assumptions what would be the resulting changes? If you were starting your business over from scratch, based on what you know now, what would you change?

Assess where your business is at right now. Consider today as your starting point. Draw up a list of your assets and liabilities. Then ask yourself the following questions and include the answers in your inventory:

- What is working the very best in your business today? What parts of your business make you the happiest?

- What's not working in your business? What causes you the most aggravation and frustration?

- What are your most important products and markets? What accounts for the largest portion of your revenues?

- Who are your most valuable people? Who are the people who account for most of your results?

- What are your special talents and skills? What is it you do that accounts for most of your success?

- What are the major changes taking place in your market? What changes should you make to compensate for them?

- What are your most treasured assumptions about your people, customers, markets, products, services and yourself? What if one of them wasn't true? What would you do then?

Bridging the gaps between what you have and what you need

Knowing where your business is at now and where you want it to be some point in the future is one thing; getting there is usually quite another. Unless you take some form of action – unless you actually do something – nothing is going to change. Execution is a thousand times more valuable than an idea.

You need to understand what gaps exist between where your business is now and where you want it to be. What pieces of the puzzle are missing? What types of people do you need? What

> **"Execution is a thousand times more valuable than an idea."**

skill-sets will they have? What actions do you need to take and what strategies or activities do you need to get involved in?

Do you even know what the gaps are? If you don't, or if you are having difficulty coming up with a list, don't worry. You are probably thinking right now that if you knew what the gaps were, you wouldn't be in this position. Understanding the gaps is the first step in creating a bridge from where you are to where you want to be – but how can you go about understanding the gaps? Where do you start? If this is making your head spin, I understand. It is normal to feel overwhelmed at this stage.

Fortunately, there is a very powerful technique that you can use to overcome this. It is called the Mastermind Group.

Mastermind

The notion of a so-called "mastermind" has probably been around for as long as people have been able to articulate their thoughts and use them to attain a goal. We have always had the belief that some people have better "brains" than others; success, therefore, seems to be the result of surrounding oneself with other "better brains." Better brains mean power and power equals success. There is nothing sinister or wrong with this.

It also should not come as a surprise that the business world has locked on to this and adapted it to meet its own ends. Back in 1937, Napoleon Hill launched his classic book *Think and*

Grow Rich and in it he devoted an entire chapter to the power of the Mastermind. Power, he wrote, is essential for success in the accumulation of money. But that's not all: power is also necessary for the retention of money after it has been accumulated.

So how does one gain power through the Mastermind? What is a Mastermind?

According to Napoleon Hill, a Mastermind may be defined as the coordination of knowledge and effort, in a spirit of harmony, between two or more people, for the attainment of a definite purpose.

In his book, Hill says that he was first introduced to the Mastermind concept by Andrew Carnegie many years before he wrote his now classic business book. Mr. Carnegie's Mastermind group, he wrote, consisted of a staff of approximately fifty men with whom he surrounded himself, for the definite purpose of manufacturing and marketing steel. Carnegie attributed his entire fortune to the power he accumulated through this Mastermind group or "brain trust."

So impressed was Hill with the whole Mastermind group concept that he said: "Do not wait (to start a Mastermind group); the time will never be 'just right'. Start where you stand, and work with whatever tools you may have at your command, and better tools will be found as you go along."

A Mastermind then is nothing more than a group of two or more people united by a definitive purpose. They benefit through interaction, cooperation and mutual contribution to themselves and to the group.

> "A Mastermind then is nothing more than a group of two or more people united by a definitive purpose. "

A Mastermind in its formal sense has a very specific make up. However, a large number of activities and structures can be used instead, such as:

- Networking organizations
- Brainstorming committees or groups
- Peer groups or affiliations
- Advisory Boards
- "Kitchen Cabinets"

Before moving on, let me explain at this point what I mean by kitchen cabinets. I came up with this concept while entertaining friends at home one day. In my house, I am the one who does all the cooking when we entertain our friends, and as a result, my friends hang out in the kitchen while I prepare the meals. We discuss life, business, the economy and just about everything else that comes to mind. Because these people are friends and people I trust, I often get some of the best, most candid advice from them. This gives rise to my concept of the Kitchen Cabinet, which is really an informal group of friends and family members I use to test ideas and brainstorm. We glean much from one another's opinions and experiences.

Such structures can be extremely powerful in any business. Sometimes a business can be completely turned around by one or two great ideas. And here I believe you need ideas that are rich in both quantity and quality: not one or the other but both. Furthermore you can gain enormously if you take heed of the power and significance of other people's perspectives. They probably see things you don't. They probably tune in to things you miss. The answers to your problems may be staring you in the face yet you simply don't see them.

It is part of the human condition to have tunnel vision. We all have experienced this from time to time, so you should be nodding your head in agreement right now as you read this. A Mastermind will help reflect various angles on your personal and professional questions.

- There are three types you would want as part of your Mastermind. They are:

- People who are in a similar environment, position or career where you can all leverage each other's resources to forward your business;

- People who operate at a level that you aspire to or who have the expertise you desire. These are the people who can give you the insights, advice and the encouragement you need to reach their position or their level of mastery. This can lead to a formal or informal type of mentorship and create networking opportunities; and,

- People who are not normally in your universe — those you would not come into contact with every day. If you're a businessperson, maybe they are more academic, artistic or scientifically oriented.

So how do you go about forming a Mastermind? It's quite simple, really. The first thing to do is to draw up a list of people whom you would ideally like to see in your Mastermind. Think about what types of expertise you would love to have in your Mastermind. This would probably be expertise that you currently don't have in your business; the type you could do with to help turn your business around.

For example, if your goal is to establish a more effective selling or marketing organization, you might want to talk to the sales and marketing manager, the vice president or highest ranking person in a given organization. Perhaps it's someone you know who has a ton of experience, expertise or an innate skill at marketing, selling or simply getting people to take action. If it is a big overall strategic or mass business growth issue that you are facing, you might want to contact the owner, the president, the general manager or the operating officer of a business near you.

Tap into people in your own social circle – perhaps you know someone who is an entrepreneur. Sometimes the best people to bounce ideas off are people who have done it on their own before, who have already succeeded in business and who have already overcome the same types of challenges you are now facing.

Start with everyone you have easy access to, and note the skill sets they possess. Contact them, introduce yourself and tell them who you are and what you do. Mention that you're turning around your business and thought it would be really great to organize a Mastermind group of people who are not competitive but complement each other well, and that he or she is someone you would be very honored to have in your group.

Once you start contacting people, I think you'll find many are very willing to be a part of something they can contribute to and receive something back in return.

> "Masterminding is the most powerful tool you have to tap into the knowledge, the minds and the methods of so many superior thinkers and business people in the world today. "

As a rule, if you can structure the Mastermind as something unique, exclusive and worth investing time in, your participants will be more than happy to be involved without tangible or financial compensation, as long as they can see immediate or long-term value in it for themselves.

Masterminding is the most powerful tool you have to tap into the knowledge, the minds and the methods of so many superior thinkers and business people in the world today. I am so convinced about this that I rate it as something you simply can't afford to be without in today's competitive marketplace.

OK, so you've now consulted widely with the people you already know, but how do you extend this concept and consult with experts you don't know or don't have access to? How can you tap into them to add to the knowledge you have already begun to build up?

Networking

Use networking as an introductory step to gain access to people you don't already know. You see, in building an organization, forming a Mastermind group or developing a network, you should be seeking diversity. Growth and learning come from contrast, not in re-enforcing what you already know. If two people agree on everything, one of you is unnecessary for change.

One of the great revolutions in the business community during the twentieth century has been the rise of networking. This occurred when companies found it expedient to 'outsource' certain jobs or functions because they were finding it difficult or expensive to attract suitable qualified staff.

So what are networks and how can you use them to turn around your business? A network is a collection of people drawn together with a view to sharing ideas and information that can be useful to you or your business. Think of them as useful contacts but remember just as you find them useful for your own ends, so too will they be looking to you to help them meet theirs. Networks are two-way streets; don't use them for what you can get out of them without being prepared to give back.

For more strategies on expanding and enhancing the effectiveness of your network go to www.the10dayturnaround.com/resources.

Networks are like marriages in that you need to work at them. Don't expect them to be blissfully harmonious. If you neglect them and only make use of them when you need them, they will let you down. You need to work at getting your networking partners to see that you are genuine about wanting to help them; to be genuinely interested in them and their businesses.

Networks are particularly powerful tools that can provide you with:

- sales advocates
- advice and ideas
- suppliers and partners
- inspiration and support

Board of Advisors

We all know what a Board of Directors is. Similarly, a small business needs to have a Board of Advisors.

A Board of Advisors is just a group of interested business experts who are willing to assist a business by offering their experience, knowledge and business wisdom. This is an invaluable business tool because most small businesses simply can't afford a Board of Directors.

Using a Board of Advisors works because it is a group of business owners and leaders getting together on a regular basis to discuss the challenges and opportunities facing each of their businesses. In this way, each represented business now has a *de facto* Board of Advisors that consists of the owners or leaders of each of them. This is a hugely valuable tool. I completely turned one of my manufacturing businesses around by introducing an advisory board. Let me explain:

Many years ago, I owned a shop fitting/signage company and we were just one of many thousands in our field of shop fitting. My goal was to be in the top five businesses in that industry, as that's where all the real money was being made. I decided that I wanted to focus on working in the toy industry.

As a parent, I knew that even if money was tight I would still buy toys for my kids and I figured most other parents would do the same, so it seemed like a recession proof area to work in. This meant working with major clients like the Walt Disney Corporation, Toys R Us, Sesame Street, Mattel and a few others. To insure that I could meet their required level of service, I invited all the CEOs and Presidents to join our advisory board.

Meetings would take place twice a year. We would supply a nice meal and over the three-hour lunch meeting we'd ask for their help, and get them to tell us what they liked and disliked about their current suppliers and what their perfect supplier would look like. Answers and suggestions flowed and we wrote as fast as we could. Then we summarized all these key insights, shared them with the group and then put an' action plan together on how our company, who wasn't actually working with most of these large corporations as yet, would put these things into practice.

It was an amazing experience, because they gave so freely of their expert advice. Within just a few months, we ended up working with all of them in a major way, because they could see our company as proactive in terms of delivering outstanding customer service. And I'm sure they also wanted to test us to see if we had made the changes they had recommended. Of course we had, so it led to us being the number one supplier to all the majors, resulting in an increase of $12 million dollars to our business in just 12 months.

If you want a sample of the letter I used to invite them to take part in the advisory board simply go to www.The10DayTurnaround. com/resources.

Another business associate of ours built a $120 million dollar home security business by listening to what the market wanted. He created an advisory board from his own employee's husbands and wives. What he did was invite all the employees life partners into the office one evening, ordered in pizzas and supplied them with wine and beer.

He wanted their feedback on what were their key frustrations, as home owners, with trade people that came to their homes. Research showed that 92% of the population had a bad experience with a tradesman in their house. Armed with this knowledge, he asked his group what things they could do as a company to create "magic moments" for the customers so the customers would feel special.

They did the following. First, he put all his employees in a uniform and made sure they were all wearing aftershave so they didn't smell. When they arrived at someone's house to fit an alarm, they would take their shoes off at the door, showing respect to the owner. His employees would carry candies and toys to give to children that were home, (only with the parents' permission of course). They would carefully put down drop sheets so no mess went onto the carpets. Before leaving the job, they would go and create little magic moments for the house owner by vacuuming a room, cleaning the glass windows, oiling squeaky doors and changing blown light bulbs. These were little extra things that weren't expected or normally a part of the tradesman's alarm installation duties.

The results were simply amazing as the home owner was always blown away with the exceptional service and therefore would tell all their friends about "the man who installed my alarm, cleaned my windows, changed the light bulbs and oiled my doors."

The moral of this story is "deliver much, much, much more than people expect" and build a business based on distinction rather than the commonplace experience.

Team Members

When assessing the present state of your business and aligning the future, one vital component to look at very carefully is the people you have in your organization.

During a turnaround, ask yourself this question: "If I were starting my business from scratch and I knew then what I know now, would I hire this person all over again?" Review each of your employees in this way, and remember that you as the business owner or leader are also a team member; employees should focus on adding value and your job as the business owner or leader must be to ensure value creation for the business's clients and market.

Assess everyone from this day forward; you can call today ground zero. You will be looking to answer questions like these:

- Who is an asset and who is a liability?
- Who can be realigned, redefined or redeployed?
- Who should be retained and who should be fired?

DAY 5: Action Checklist

You're half way home to your turnaround transformation. Determining the best way to get from where you are to where you want to go begins with understanding exactly where you are. Knowing what needs to change, what should stay the same, and understanding exactly what you have to work with in terms of skills, resources, challenges, and opportunities is key to creating a well-thought-out plan of action to move forward.

☑ Completed reading Day 5.

☐ Answer the 12 questions to describe my current business.

☐ Answer the questions relating to my business as it will be 3 to 6 months into the future.

☐ Complete the "gut feel" exercise.

☐ Create a to-do list of activities to begin my plan for change.

☐ Start my to-do list, monitor and measure my results.

☐ Decide what can be outsourced or eliminated from my to-do list based on my results.

☐ Create the asset inventory and liability list.

☐ Make a list of people who are ideal for a Mastermind group.

☐ Send emails to those individuals inviting them to join a Mastermind group.

☐ Take one step in networking.

☐ Assess everyone using team member criteria.

☐ Download the sample letter for advisory boards at www.The10DayTurnaround.com

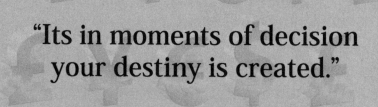

"Its in moments of decision
your destiny is created."

Darren J Stephens
International Bestselling Author & Speaker

Chapter 6

Day 6

The 10 DAY TURNAROUND

Planning Key Actions

Chapter 6
Planning Key Actions

It's Day 6. You've passed the halfway mark and you're heading home!

I just love what Jack Welch once said. According to him, an organization's ability to learn, and to translate that learning into action, is the ultimate competitive advantage. Action must accompany insight.

Taking Action

"Vision without action is a daydream. Action without vision is a nightmare." Japanese Proverb

> **"Nothing will happen unless you take action."**

In business, just as in life, nothing will happen unless you take action. You have to actually do something to cause something to change, to move or to accelerate or slow down. Nothing happens spontaneously.

If we do nothing, then nothing is going to happen. If you are seeking different business results from those you have been getting until now, then you have to do something different from what you have been doing in business until now. You see, if you continue doing the same things you have always done, then you should expect to get the same results that you have been getting until now.

There's no use doing what you have always done if you want to turn your business around. You have to change and overcome any resistance to change – and there will be resistance. People looking to change face internal resistance inside their company and inside themselves. They often face the pressure of the status quo and the patterns of the past that hold them back. The weight of change can be heavy.

Using leverage is a great way to overcome resistance to change. Yet the key to leverage isn't just about the length of the lever and the fulcrum. It's also about knowing where you stand. This leverage could be a new strategy or it could be getting other people to assist in supporting the change. It could also be approaching something in a completely different way so as to avoid the opposing forces or escape or eliminate the current conditions all together.

If you understand the forces at play here and what you need to use them to your advantage, then you have every chance of succeeding in anything you do.

Why is it that some people seem to succeed at everything they tackle while others don't? Is it that they were born lucky? Of course not. Is it because they are wealthy? Again, this is illogical because many of the most successful people are not rich. And when you look into it, most of the world's largest and most successful companies started with little or no money. Is it because they are naturally positive? Now we may be getting closer to the truth. There certainly is plenty of evidence to suggest that one's outlook has a lot to do with one's achievements.

Mindset is another way of describing one's outlook. Experience has shown that you certainly need to work on your mindset just as much as you do your business and that without a positive mindset, you will find it exceedingly difficult to turn any business around. It will be just about impossible in a short ten days without the right mindset.

What frame of mind are you in right now? Positive? Excited? Apprehensive? Worried? Nervous? Panic-stricken? Or overwhelmed?

How are you going to move into the mental space you know you need to be in to undertake this turnaround process? What do you need to do? Who do you need to speak with? What do you have to put in place?

Your Three Most Important Goals

> "When it is obvious that the goals cannot be reached,
> don't adjust the goals, adjust the action steps."
> Confucius

What are the three most important goals you have for yourself and your business? Why are they important? When you accomplish these goals what will it give you, your business, your clients and customers and your market?

When you have accomplished these goals what will your business look like and how will it perform? How will you know when you have accomplished these goals, individually and collectively? How will you measure your progress in moving toward these goals?

What will you observe, experience or measure both qualitatively and quantitatively?

What will you have to do, give or get to achieve these goals? What can you do starting right now?

Managing your time, your talent and your resources

As a responsible turnaround manager, your job must be to encourage your team to do what they do best. Make sure they have all the tools they will need for the job or task you expect them to do.

Let your team members know what you expect of them. It sounds basic, but you'd be surprised by the number of employees who simply don't know what they are expected to do or at what level they are expected to perform.

Recognize work well done. There is nothing more motivating than that. It shows you care about your team, and so you should. But let them know it, too!

Also encourage their personal development. Show them you value their contribution and that what they are doing really does make a difference. Value their jobs just as much as you value their contribution.

Encourage collaboration, shared interests and trust between your team members. They do, after all, spend the majority of their lives at work, working for you. Evaluate their efforts and give them constructive, honest feedback.

As a turnaround leader, you also need to ensure that you don't spend all your time managing your team so that you forget to manage yourself; your time and your own skills and resources. You need to ensure everything is kept in perspective. The outcome of this program will be depending on it.

The Art of the Start

> "Races are won and lost in the starting blocks."

In sports, most races are won and lost at the starting blocks. The way the athlete springs into action at the starting gun is everything. There are some well-documented examples of exceptionally talented disabled runners who are actually faster runners than many of their high-profile able-bodied colleagues, yet they can never quite beat them on the track. The reason for this lies in the starts. A runner with an artificial leg simply can't explode out of the starting blocks as quickly as an able-bodied athlete can.

In business it is just the same. And when working on turning around a business, this is particularly true.

> "Clarity of mind, decisiveness and strong leadership are the keys."

When you are engaged in the turnaround process, time is of the essence. For this reason, clarity of mind, decisiveness and strong leadership are the keys. Without these, you will simply not have what it takes to deal with Newton's three laws of motion.

The 10 Day Turnaround is all about building enough momentum up to set things in motion. It's all about new beginnings, striving for new goals, energizing everyone concerned and doing whatever it takes. This is a time when strong leadership is called for. That's because every single team member will be required to pull together with maximum effort so that, together, their combined effort will create the forward motion necessary to achieve a turnaround.

A lack of action is perhaps the biggest single issue facing business today. And it is not surprising then, that those that execute well are always far more robust businesses that are able to respond to changing marketplace conditions.

Executing turnaround plans involve three key processes: people processes, strategy processes and operations processes. All are equally important. It's also vital that the business has the right leader to lead the turnaround process. And by this I mean a leader who is mentally up to the task.

I will explain more about this in a moment, but first it is important to realize that in order to succeed, the business, too, must have certain attributes.

It needs hands-on leaders who understand the turnaround process, it needs to have a corporate culture that values the whole process, and it needs the right team members in the right positions.

The art of the start implies that the business has the right team members focusing on the right details at the right time.

Okay, let's get back to the leader now. When I say the business must have the right leader, I mean it must have a leader who appreciates the fact that the ultimate result will depend on his or her subscribing to the art of the start.

What does this mean? It simply means that the leader must follow the straightforward process of getting into action quickly and effectively. This is vital because, being a condensed 10 day period that we are talking about, the leader's role is pivotal. For more information about the leverage of leadership and "The Eight Great Mistakes of Leadership" go to www.The10DayTurnaround. com/resources.

> "It is time to begin to make it a reality."

During Day 6, you will be aiming to begin to move from the vision stage to the execution phase of your turnaround plan. Now that you have a vision for something greater, it is time to begin to make it a reality.

What are the three most important decisions you could make or transformative actions you could take today to get things moving? What are the sub-steps necessary? In order to have your intention and desires come to fruition, what must you start doing? What must you stop doing? What must you do more of or less of? What is the sequence of action steps you need to take?

These are the sorts of questions that you should be mulling over in your mind as you prepare to take action.

To simplify matters and create sense out of confusion, take a sheet of paper and write down the following main headings, and then complete, in as much detail as you can, answers to the memory joggers alongside each.

Intentions: What is it that you are intending to do?

_____

_____

_____

_____

Assumptions: What do you assume to be true about the current situation? What do you believe the benefits to be of what you are intending? Why do you believe it to be necessary or desirable? Why do you think it is possible, probable or certain that it can be done? What are your assumptions about the resources necessary and available to transform your intention into reality?

_____

_____

_____

_____

Decisions: What needs to change from the current situation in order to have your intention fulfilled? What resources are needed and which of those resources do you currently have available? How will you obtain or allocate the resources necessary to begin and sustain the new direction or changes?

_____

_____

_____

_____

_____

Actions: What are all the actions or activities necessarily involved in moving toward your intention? What are the primary activities to get started? What are the on-going activities and actions necessary to continue the progress toward your goal?

_____

_____

_____

_____

Accountabilities: What needs to be done and in what order, by whom, and when? What won't have to be done? How will success and progress be measured? What are the methods of management, communication and feedback in the process of implementation?

What you will have now is a concise snapshot of your turnaround process. What you need now is a little more detailed discussion of some of the steps involved in the process itself. I call it "10 easy steps to a turnaround," and they are the following:

1. Adjust your mindset
2. Create a turnaround plan of action
3. Get rid of fear – fear of failure as well as success
4. Ramp up your energy level
5. Push yourself relentlessly – it will only last for 10 days
6. Create the right physical environment – something inspirational and stimulating
7. Lead by positive reinforcement – use a carrot, not a stick
8. Master your time – you don't have much of it, so use it well

> 9. Test and measure everything – so you know how you are tracking
> 10. Deal effectively with excuses – they are going to come on thick and fast

Before looking at the art of the start in more detail, it's important for you to take the time now to make sure you comprehend the above ten points. Make a list of them, tick them off to indicate that they now apply to you, and pin the list up in a prominent place at your desk. Refer to them first thing in the morning from here on in, as well as last thing at night. Make sure you do this each and every day because you really want to insure that these 10 items become like a mantra to you.

Now to the process of the art of the start. This is key to beginning a successful turnaround process in a short 10 day period and it consists of 8 distinct activities that you are going to need to master.

The 8 Key Activities

1. ***Get out of the gate***. The first thing you need to do is to make a start. It's no use mulling over progress reports, projected figures, plans and goals; the important thing to do is to just get the ball rolling. Inactivity leads to procrastination and this is the biggest enemy of any business owner or leader. Get up, get out, and get moving. A good idea started is better than a perfected idea still on the drawing board. Get things happening right now; you can review your current situation, your intended goals and the plans you have to get there as you go. Once you're in motion, start

work on redefining your business and developing, testing, and measuring strategies and tools. Remember, you need movement to get momentum and from momentum you can gain velocity and ultimately critical mass in any endeavor—but it won't start unless you do.

2. ***Jockeying for position.*** Once you are out of the starting gate, you need to position your business on the right track to success. What you will be aiming to do here is to differentiate your business from your competitors. Look closely at the things that set you apart from your competition. What makes doing business with you and your company a unique experience? What benefits or solutions does your company provide that makes you *the obvious choice* for a prospect to spend their money with? What you will be aiming to achieve during this stage is telling your clients why they should or must do business with you instead of your competition and telling any prospective team members why they should want to work for you. Look at every one of the details. Then, take a step back and take a larger look around.

3. ***Finding new business.*** Every successful business needs a group of possible customers you can identify and reach, with a problem they want to fix using your solution, and the desire and ability to spend their money to meet their need. Business is like a sausage machine; you need to keep feeding it with new prospects. It's a continual process. It's also an important one.

In searching for new business you have to stand up and standout in a hurry. Attention spans are short, and the selection of products and services are virtually unlimited. To get noticed you have to be uniquely suited and clearly defined in the mind of the marketplace and the eyes of your prospects.

Remember, you don't have the luxury of time now, so these are your priorities: explain yourself and what you do in 60 seconds to everyone you meet and everyone you can reach; have great answers to questions about your value and purpose; understand your target market inside-out; and develop a great presentation that is concise and to-the-point and focused on solving problems and delivering benefits for your prospects and customers. Have something meaningful to say, say it well, say it quickly, and say it often.

4. *Create a strategic "to do" and "to don't" list.* Lists and plans keep the team focused and pointing in the same direction, but they are not everything. Taking action counts more, but taking the right action means everything; remember "right action creates right results". Look for things that are easy to implement and have the greatest relative impact on your business in the shortest time possible. Go on a low information diet and learn how to separate the extraneous from the essential and focus on what's important right now.

5. *Think big but start small.* Conserve cash where you can, focus on efficiencies, effectiveness, and eliminating constraints wherever and whenever you are able. Seek out small or quick "wins" and rack 'em up. Look for windfall profit opportunities in your business such as reactivating your inactive clients or getting your customers to buy sooner, longer, more often, or larger quantities. Find ways to create urgency in your buyer base and develop ways to offer more value to your past, current, and future customers. Create and implement a referral program for your current customers or create a "frequent-buyer" program to get them to buy today instead of tomorrow.

6. ***Evaluate everyone inside and outside your organization.*** Evaluate your team to make sure you have the right talent on your team. Look to update and upgrade the knowledge base within your company. Take a hard look at your clients and decide if they are worth the money you earn providing them your service or product. Rank your customers in terms of bottom line contribution as well as top line revenue—some clients cost more to serve than the money you make in servicing them. (The customer is always right but sometimes they are "right" for someone else other than your company.)

7. ***Partner for Profit.*** Look for opportunities to partner up with others by creating strategic alliances, cross promotions, product bundling, bartering, or creating "joint-ventures". Ask yourself "Who else stands to gain by my survival and success?" Make a list of those people and find a way to create value for them and ask for their support in return. Perhaps they can introduce your company, product, or service to their customer-base. Maybe you can combine your product or a service with someone else's to make a new "offering" to the market. Perhaps you can trade some of your products, services, or expertise for something you need from someone else—get creative, get going, and keep moving forward.

8. ***Branding.*** Create a great brand for your business by getting people excited! Allow them to test your products before buying. Involve your customers as soon as possible, as it produces feelings of familiarity and ease in their buying habits. Encourage them to tell others by word of mouth; don't leave it to chance— ask your current and past buyers to recommend you to their family, friends, clients, and colleagues. Engage your personal and professional network to introduce you to new markets and

prospects. Use social media to spread the word about you and your company. Create a Facebook page, create a Twitter account, and get the buzz out.

Remember, you must be willing to do whatever it takes! Find out how to get your company, your products, your service, and yes—YOU out in front of as many people as possible. Do something out of the ordinary or even outrageous in comparison to your competition and get noticed. Great brands create raving fans and great brands are built through visibility, credibility and distinction.

Don't Just Do Anything, Do The Right Thing

In turning around a business, what we are essentially looking to achieve is change. But not just any change; we are looking for specific change – change that will take the business in a particular direction. This is what all your vision-making, planning and execution phase implementation is all about.

In order to make your vision a reality—to move your intentions into action—something has to change from the current state. Every change involves making decisions and taking action. But where do you start?

Some time ago I came across a model for change in my friend Brian Tracy's work. I was impressed. The more I thought about it, the more I realized I couldn't improve upon it and so adopted it and used it many times over. He called it the four methods of change.

The Four Methods of Change

Remember the four different types of making a change, as we mentioned earlier. They include:

1. Start doing something you're not currently doing
2. Stop doing something you're currently doing
3. Do more of something you're currently doing
4. Do less of something you're currently doing

Start at the Beginning

In implementing any plan or strategy, you have to get started. Starting might be easy but starting smart is also key. You might have a plan with infinite potential, but every business has a finite amount of resources and as a business leader, you have a limited amount of time, energy and attention. How you allocate your resources has as much to do with the likely outcome of your plan as the plan itself. How you order and sequence what needs to be done can determine whether you turn your business around in a month or in a hundred years.

Most Impactful, Meaningful, Measurable, Observable Steps

In prioritizing your actions and activities, evaluate everything according to the following items:

Significance: What is the strategic impact upon your business?

Probability: What's the likelihood of success or completion?

Immediacy: Can it be done starting now?

Sustainability: Can it be continued over time?

Scalability: Can it be leveraged or increased (carried out by other people, more often, in other areas, or across other activities)?

Aligning Decisions and Actions to Income

The final point to bear in mind at this stage is that all your decisions and actions need to be aligned to meet desired income levels. You see, the whole point of needing to turn a business around is to produce a better result, and that invariably relates to income.

The basic aim of business, any business, is and has always been to produce a profit. Profitability is a necessity because without it the business would wither and die. Income, or cash flow, is the lifeblood of business and as such, income must remain at the forefront of your mind.

"Keep going! You're doing an awesome job and you're over halfway there!"

DAY 6: Action Checklist

The best way to change your results begins with changing your actions. The best way to change your actions is to change your mind-set. You're moving into the homestretch and as Zig Ziglar is famous for saying "It's time for a check-up from the neck-up." Take the time to think, plan and prioritize what you're committed to doing. You are well on your way to transforming your business and your life for the better, forever.

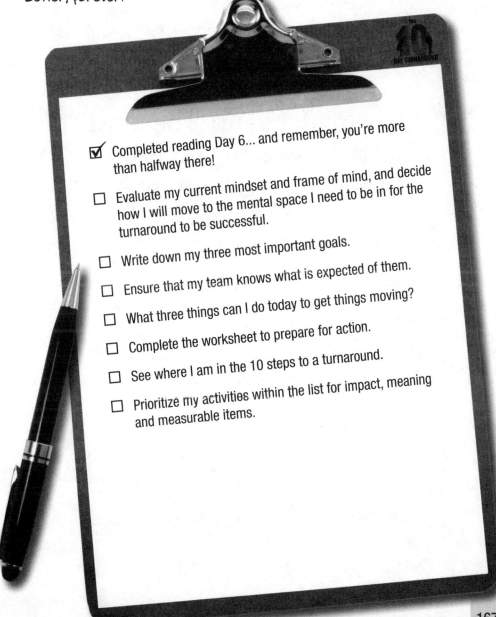

☑ Completed reading Day 6... and remember, you're more than halfway there!

☐ Evaluate my current mindset and frame of mind, and decide how I will move to the mental space I need to be in for the turnaround to be successful.

☐ Write down my three most important goals.

☐ Ensure that my team knows what is expected of them.

☐ What three things can I do today to get things moving?

☐ Complete the worksheet to prepare for action.

☐ See where I am in the 10 steps to a turnaround.

☐ Prioritize my activities within the list for impact, meaning and measurable items.

"Our greatest weakness lies in giving up. The most certain way to succeed is always to try just one more time."

Thomas A. Edison
Winner, Nobel Prize for Physics

Chapter 7

Day 7

The 10 DAY TURNAROUND

"Core" Fitness

Chapter 7
"Core" Fitness

The longest work-week of your career so far? Perhaps. The most rewarding? Without question!

Strengthen the Core

Things will be moving now! In order to lead your business in the desired direction, you now need to roll your sleeves up and take a more hands-on role.

It is time to zero-in on the inner workings of your business. It is time to take a closer look at the very core of your business.

But before we get into specifics, let's consider for a moment what a "core" is. Generally speaking, the core of a business is the central, most essential part. Think of it this way: if you were to remove the core of a business, the business would no longer be recognizable as that business. Take Shell for instance, a company with over $458 billion in revenues. We all know Shell as an oil company but it is also involved in a whole host of other businesses like chemicals, exploration, transportation and more. If they were to shut down the oil side of their business, they would be unrecognizable as Shell, wouldn't they?

And sure, Shell has weathered tough times over the years. So how did they survive? They strengthened their core business and got out of diversified businesses in order to expand their strengths.

This reminds me of some words of wisdom from Jack Welch: if you don't have a competitive advantage, then don't compete. Business often do what they do "worst" first hoping to get better while they take for granted what they do well. In fact, most companies spend more time propping up their weakness than concentrating on their strengths. This weakens the core until eventually the company or the organization collapses.

There are two basic ways of going about strengthening your core:

1. You could move towards that which you do best or;
2. You could move away from that which you do worst.

The end result may be the same but it's a matter of what works best for you. Do what you do best "the most" and what you do worst "the least."

Expanding Your Strengths

Think of the core of your business as being what you excel at. It is your reason for being in business. This is your strength. Take the time now to write down what your strengths in business are. One sentence will do. Make it a statement of fact.

My strengths are: _____

_____

_____

_____

Reflect on this statement a little by reading it over and over as you visualize what it means. Do you understand it to mean that you are very good at what you do? Is the language positive and empowering? Is it unambiguous? Do you believe it is true?

The more you think about it, the more you will discover that you actually have more strengths than you may have written down at first. You see, you have strengths at two main levels; there is the external level – the main purpose of your business – and strengths at an internal level – skills that reside within the business at the team level.

At the external level, your strength may very well be your unique selling proposition. It is likely to be what sets you apart from your competition and gives you the marketing edge you need to prosper.

At the internal level, it may be the core strengths you have within the business that allow you to not only stay in business, but to stay one step ahead of your competition. It may be things like specific skills or craftsmanship that your business has, it may be systems and technology, or it may be intangibles like goodwill and a respected presence in the marketplace.

So what are your internal strengths? Make a note of as many of them now as you can:

My internal strengths are:

1. _____

2. _____

3. _____

4. _____
5. _____
6. _____
7. _____
8. _____
9. _____
10. _____

Your task now during Day 7 of your 10 Day Turnaround program is to expand your strengths. Of course, it is difficult to expand or improve something if you don't know the extent of it. How will you know if what you have put in place is an improvement?

Have a good look at your strengths, now. Do you see any patterns appearing? Are all of your strengths in one particular area? Are there any obvious gaps or omissions that you can see?

Maximize and Multiply

"Maximize your strengths."

The first thing you need to do now is maximize your strengths. What can you add to from your list? What can you enhance? Are there any skills that need updating or adding to? Are there any team members who could be cross-trained? Are there any skill-sets you could take up that would add to skills you already have? Can you put more time and energy into supporting your best, most profitable clients, operations, products or services? How about concentrating your strengths in a single location instead of having them spread throughout the organization?

The advantage of maximizing your strengths is that it will cause your effectiveness to multiply. By strengthening your core, you will see benefits that are disproportionate to the sum of the individual strengths themselves. The results are cumulative and add powerfully to your bottom line.

Take the time now to make a note of the strengths you will maximize within your business.

Strengths to maximize include:

1. _____
2. _____
3. _____
4. _____
5. _____

Overcoming Your Weaknesses

The other important way to strengthen your core is, of course, to overcome your weaknesses. By overcoming or eliminating your weaknesses, you will be left with just your strengths.

This is the other side of the coin and it is equally relevant. However, some people respond better to being pushed than pulled. The end result may be the same, but the motivation differs. It's just a matter of understanding what works best for you.

So what are your weaknesses? Make a note of as many of them now as you can.

My weaknesses are:

1. _____
2. _____
3. _____
4. _____
5. _____
6. _____
7. _____
8. _____
9. _____
10. _____

You'll want to focus on overcoming these weaknesses. Just as it's difficult to improve on your strengths without really understanding the extent of them, how do you eliminate or overcome something if you don't know the extent of it? How will you know if what you have put in place is an improvement?

Have a good look at your weaknesses, now. Do you see any patterns appearing? Are all your weaknesses in one particular area? Are there any obvious groupings or trends that you can see?

Minimize and Divide

Have a good look at your lists now. Can you easily eliminate a group of weaknesses in one move? Will the elimination or minimization of one lead to a domino effect with others? Can you redirect some to enhance others and so get rid of an unwanted weakness?

The power of minimization lies in its eventual effect; it works like division and not subtraction. Minimizing a weakness has a compound effect as far as the end result is concerned. Minimizing your weaknesses is like multiplying your strengths.

Take the time now to make a note of the weaknesses you will minimize within your business.

Weaknesses to minimize include:

1. _____
2. _____
3. _____
4. _____
5. _____

If you'd like to complete an analysis of your strengths, weaknesses, opportunities, and threats (S.W.O.T.) facing your business go to www.the10dayturnaround.com/resources.

Eliminate Constraints

Constraints can be debilitating to any business. They can interfere with the normal flow of events and eventually stifle your cash flow.

Think of what happens to your garden hose when you turn on the tap. Water flows out of the nozzle. What happens if you twist the hose back on itself? The flow of water will diminish.

This is because what you have done by putting a kink in the hose is place a constraint on the hose. The moment you eliminate the constraint by straightening out the hose again, the water begins to flow normally again.

Of course, this isn't the only type of constraint you can place on the hose. You could twist the nozzle spout and cause the water to flow slower, or faster. You could block the end of the nozzle with your finger and stop the flow of water all together.

But there's another thing that may be even more troubling to gardeners; sometimes they don't even know their hose has a constraint! They suspect the water pressure isn't what it should be, and it is only when they investigate that they discover the hose is twisted. A quick untwisting restores the water flow to its full potential.

Do you know whether your business has any constraints that are preventing it from reaching its full potential? And if you suspect there are, do you know exactly what they are? How can you find out?

> **"Constraints are the inherent risks in a system."**

Constraints are the inherent risks in a system limiting the ability or capacity for growth. Like the twisted garden hose reducing water flow, until you eliminate, reduce, overcome or avoid the existing or inherent constraints in your business or your business model, you'll never achieve your highest level of performance or reach your full potential.

In order to eliminate, reduce, overcome or avoid the constraints in your business your first challenge is to identify what they are. What's holding you back? If you were to increase your business activity or revenue by 5, 10, or 25% what would have to change? How can you make those changes now? What else will be affected, either positively or negatively? When you overcome these current limitations, what will it mean for your business strategically or financially?

Constraints may be a lack of resources such as capital, talent, expertise, equipment or customers. Constraints could also be your time, your attention, or your ability to focus. Your business could be held back by a constraint on your vision, your planning or your ability to lead, direct and manage. Constraints can be internal, external, simple or complex, fixed or fluid.

Matt Clarkson, whom I mentioned in an earlier chapter, had a major constraint in his business, which was stopping his growth. As an expert marketer and through the power of the internet he was generating over 100 new leads a day in his business. The problem he had was to be able to hire and train enough sales people to follow up all the hot leads. His sales team was complaining they had too many leads and asking him to stop the marketing activities. You can imagine him as the business owner saying no to increased sales.

I remember him telling me that in his frustration he told his team, "Don't tell me to slow down the lead flow, you guys just need to catch up." At this time he was faced with a few constraints. The other one being that he'd run out of office space and he was even running split shifts in the office, allowing some of the team to work from home on some days while someone else would use their desk to follow up the sales leads on that day.

Eventually he decided to overcome the two constraints by franchising his Bidding Buzz eBay business, which allowed him to expand the sales team much more rapidly and grow the business exponentially.

Develop a dual strategy to busting through your current constraints. First, look for the constraints that have the highest amount of negative leverage in your business or your business model and develop a strategy to overcome those. Secondly, develop a focus to predict and avoid constraints to your future growth and avoid them before they occur.

<u>Remember that execution</u> is a thousand times
more valuable than an idea!

"Well done!
You only have
3 days to go,
so keep up the
great work."

DAY 7: Action Checklist

Today's chapter was short, not by default but by design. It's easy to read, less easy to complete. Make sure to make the time and take the time to complete the following items on the checklist. Without an objective assessment, recognition, appreciation and understanding of what you're working with, what you offer and what you're facing, making lasting change is virtually impossible. There's a place inside us all where dreams come true and obstacles fall and it begins with right here.

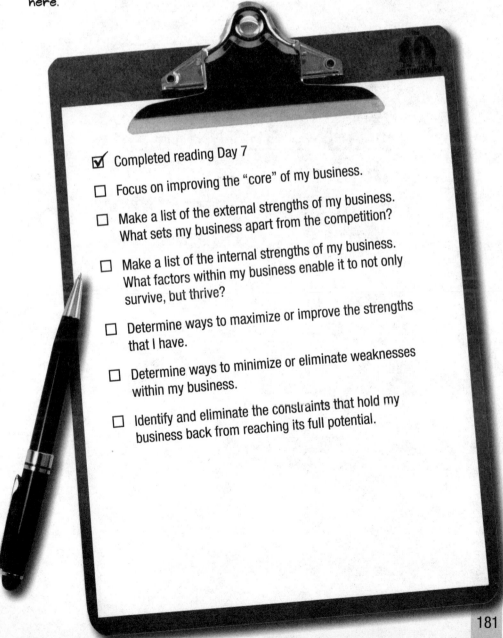

☑ Completed reading Day 7

☐ Focus on improving the "core" of my business.

☐ Make a list of the external strengths of my business. What sets my business apart from the competition?

☐ Make a list of the internal strengths of my business. What factors within my business enable it to not only survive, but thrive?

☐ Determine ways to maximize or improve the strengths that I have.

☐ Determine ways to minimize or eliminate weaknesses within my business.

☐ Identify and eliminate the constraints that hold my business back from reaching its full potential.

"An expert is someone who has succeeded in making decisions and judgments simpler through knowing what to pay attention to and what to ignore."

Edward de Bono
International Bestselling Author

Chapter 8

Day 8

The 10 DAY TURNAROUND

Making The Right Decisions

Chapter 8
Making The Right Decisions

You've worked so hard over the past seven days, and we congratulate you for your dedication to your own future and the future of your business. Just a few more days, and then you'll have completed the entire process. Your business will run more effectively than ever... and you'll have a new skill set as a "turnaround expert" that you can apply to other businesses. We promised you that ability... and we're sure that by now, you see that you'll have it, too!

Winston Churchill said, "The optimist sees opportunity in every danger; the pessimist sees danger in every opportunity." Are you optimistic regarding your business operations – or does your pessimism hold you back?

Question Everything

A primary role of being a business leader is having to make decisions. The interesting thing about this is that it is two-fold: first it is a matter of actually making the decision and secondly, the matter of making the *right* decision.

Let's look at these two aspects separately.

Many business leaders find it extremely difficult and stressful to make a decision. They end up committing one of business' cardinal sins – procrastination.

Procrastination is a symptom of indecision. It is a distraction; it's counter-productive and sometimes catastrophic. As Peter F. Drucker said, "A degenerative disease will not be cured by procrastination." It requires decisive change.

> **"It's often better to do the wrong thing than to do nothing at all."**

It's often better to do the wrong thing than to do nothing at all. You see, it is usually easy to correct a wrong move but a missed opportunity may never come again.

Making decisions is all about taking action. It involves doing something, even if it is only a mental activity. It is this act of doing something that scares many people, yet it doesn't need to. It really does take just as much effort to do something as it takes to do nothing at all – yet the results are often light years apart.

> **"Making decisions is all about taking action."**

When you do nothing, you can experience more stress than when you do *something*. This is because by doing something, you set your mind at ease. It allows you to move on and not worry about the process of making a decision; you can use your energy more effectively on other issues waiting for your attention.

The thing that gets in the way for many business leaders when it comes to taking action or not is that they confuse the two aspects of making decisions. They are afraid they will choose the wrong course of action and make a costly mistake. If what you are already doing isn't getting you the results you want, however, doing

> "Movement creates feedback and makes progress from the status quo."

something else will at the very least rule out the wrong course of action. Movement creates feedback and makes progress from the status quo— if you discover you've gone the wrong way changing direction is easier than getting started.

As General George Patton once said, "A good plan implemented today is better than a perfect plan implemented tomorrow." He knew very well that hanging on until something is perfect is just another form of procrastination and a reason to delay taking action. He knew that part two of the process – getting it right – mustn't get in the way of getting things moving.

Great leaders are known for their ability to make decisions and take action. They are people who aren't afraid to do something, even if it turns out not to be the right thing at first.

Taking action should come easy to you, the business leader. It should be something that you do naturally. This makes it easy to implement. Just do something next time something needs to be done.
The next part of the decision-making equation isn't so easy. It involves making the RIGHT decision.

How do you go about doing that? How do you even begin to evaluate all your options and courses of action, without falling back to procrastinating and avoiding action, especially when you are in a turnaround situation?

Challenge Your Assumptions

Even though the best plans are based on a set of assumptions, it doesn't mean that they will be correct. Assumptions are just that: best guesses or beliefs based on circumstances that might not still be in effect.

One of the characteristics of assumptions is that they tend to change over time. This is because everything changes. We do, after all, live in a dynamic and ever-changing world.

What works one day may not the next. Furthermore, if it worked one day why should it the next? Things change. Markets change, people's preferences change and the needs of customers and clients are fluid. Think about this: the number of choices you have today as a consumer are exponentially expanded from the choices you had five years ago.

This doesn't mean to say that what's working for your business right now shouldn't work in the future; rather, you could be limiting your potential by not challenging your basic business assumptions. If you were running a business that sold carbon paper thirty years ago you would have had a good, viable business. But if you hadn't challenged your basic assumption that the consumption of carbon paper would continue to grow each year, you would have been in serious trouble just a few short years down the track once the personal computer gained a foothold in the market. You could have found a way to make the carbon paper cheaper, faster, with better quality and with more choices for the market and still your business would be obsolete. Efficient — but obsolete, just the same.

You need to challenge the things you assume about your environment as well. Take a good hard look at your people too. Are they the right ones for the needs of your organization today and the challenges that lie ahead? They may have been good when times were good, but during a turnaround period, can they produce the results in the time frame that you need? Are they up to the challenges that lie ahead?

Challenging Your Assumptions

Challenge your assumptions about your business model. Look at what's working and what's not. I remember working with a business that was experiencing a sharp fall in revenue. This business happened to have a very complicated sales process, and when sales began to fall off, instead of looking internally and questioning their systems, they spent thousands on trying to develop new markets. The result, of course, was that they strangled their cash flow.

Have a good look at your assumptions about the marketplace and ask yourself if your clients really do need what you supply.

Challenge your day-to-day operations. My experience shows that when customers stop buying, most business leaders assume it is because they have found a better price elsewhere. In fact, what has invariably happened is that they had merely forgotten about the business in question - simply because that business had forgotten about them and failed to keep in touch, or lost the ability to provide what the market wants or needs today.

Thinking Outside-the-Box and Inside-the-Box

Every business owner is familiar with the term and concept of thinking outside of the box. Let's talk about how to make these expressions more than timeworn clichés.

When faced with a turnaround situation, you really have to look first inside the box at the things you are currently doing in the business. Most business leaders make the mistake of jumping to the conclusion that because they are no longer getting the results they want, they need to instigate new methods of generating cash flow. They try opening new markets or developing new products. Or they launch a new marketing campaign.

What they should be doing first is taking a good, hard look at what they are currently doing to see if they can do things better, faster or smoother. They should be looking to improve efficiencies and economies of scale within their current business activities.

Once they have done this, then it would be appropriate to begin looking outside the box. By this, I mean taking a detailed look at what is done in other industries or businesses. Just because players in one industry do things in a particular way doesn't mean that those in other industries can't do something similar and get good results.

Over the years, I have found that there is a general misunderstanding among business leaders when it comes to optimization and innovation. They get the two confused, with similar effects on their businesses.

Optimization is about doing what you are already doing, but doing it better. It is about working inside-the-box.

Innovation, on the other hand, is all about doing things differently; it is about working outside-the-box. Innovation involves leadership. Innovation is the act of introducing something new.

Neither entrepreneurship nor innovation can exist without initiative and a willingness to do something differently.

Innovation is at the heart of progress and the center of entrepreneurship. Innovation is in the soul of change, growth and improvement. Any conscious and dramatic shift in a business, company, market, product, service or system requires initiative, planning and managed innovation.

Peter Drucker, probably the preeminent authority on leadership was also a leading advocate and voice of innovation. In his book *Innovation and Entrepreneurship*, Drucker details seven areas to explore for innovative opportunities, which are worth mentioning here.

1. ***The Unexpected.*** An unexpected success, an unanticipated failure, or an unpredicted outside event can be a sign or a symptom of a unique opportunity. The unexpected indicates a deviation from the norm, something outside of the plan, process, practice or procedure. In analyzing the unexpected, you can uncover something unique that can be modeled, duplicated, enhanced or eliminated.

2. ***The Incongruous***. A discrepancy between reality and common perception. Any disconnect between what 'is' and

what everyone assumes it to be or what it ought to be can create an innovative opportunity.

3. *A Process Need.* When a weak link is evident in a particular process, often people work around it or compensate for it instead of doing something about it. Strengthening, supplementing, avoiding or eliminating the weak link is an innovation opportunity for a person, product, service or company.

4. ***Changes in an Industry, Market Structure or Economy.*** The invitation or need for an innovative product, service or business model or approach occurs when the underlying foundation or conditions of an industry, market or economy shifts. Recognizing the change and being the first to innovate is often the key to survival and success.

5. ***Demographics.*** Changes in the population's size, age structure, composition, employment, level of education and income can create innovative opportunities. Predicting the logical outcome of a change or trend can allow innovative products, services and companies to meet the changing needs and tastes of a fluid population.

6. ***Psychographics or Changes in Perception, Mood and Meaning in a Market.*** Innovation opportunities often exist when a society's general assumptions, attitudes, tastes, preferences, desires or beliefs change. Recognizing the perceptual shifts, the evolving tone, or changing mood of a market, culture or population segment can allow you to set and direct the trend and fill the new needs and desires.

7. ***New Knowledge or Technology***. Advances in technology, scientific and non-scientific knowledge can create needs for new products and services and generate new markets. As people and populations learn more, they want more, need more and can do more. Greater knowledge increases an awareness of new choices and possibilities.

Looking for, finding, and using these seven areas of innovation and opportunity, and exercising the entrepreneurial initiative to create something new, different, better or unique is the greatest security and avenue of success for any business or individual.

Once the opportunity for innovation has been discovered, Drucker recommends using these five steps to convert the opportunity into reality.

1. Begin with an analysis of the opportunity—what is it, who is it for, why would they want it, what would they be willing to pay for it, etc?

2. Evaluate the market potential to see if people will be interested in using the innovation.

3. To be effective, the innovation must be simple and focused on a specific need or desire of a market segment.

4. Most effective innovations start out small. By appealing to a small, limited market, a product or service requires little capital and risk and only a few people to produce and sell it. As the market expands, the company has time to expand and fine-tune its processes and stay ahead of the competition.

5. Aim and strive for market leadership. If an innovation or the innovator does not aim at leadership in the beginning, it is unlikely to be innovative enough to successfully establish itself. Market leadership can mean long-term domination of a small market niche.

Innovation and entrepreneurial initiative are keys to long-lasting business success in an integrated global economy. Optimization can be used to service an existing market more cost-effectively and should always remain a management and operational priority. Effective innovation and the willingness to do, develop and deliver something new, better or unique will ensure the significance of a business for the longest period of time possible.

> "Market leadership can mean long-term domination of a small market niche.
>
> Innovation and entrepreneurial initiative are keys to long-lasting business success."

Optimization often comes from modeling what someone else in your market or industry is doing and finding a way to do it somewhat better. Generally, innovation comes from looking at something that someone else is doing in another industry and adapting it to, or in, your own business.

When trying to find breakthroughs and innovation, don't just look in your business, at your competition or in your industry — that's not usually where breakthroughs occur. You need to look further than that. Learn from the outside and implement from the inside. You optimize from the inside and innovate from the outside.

So can you draw parallels with your industry and others? Can you take a leaf out of their book and adapt it to yours? Let's look at a few examples.

Netflix, the monthly DVD subscription service company, modeled what was essentially used for more than a hundred years by book libraries. Federal Express applied the existing passenger airline 'hub-and-spoke' model to overnight delivery. Amazon adopted the 'just-in-time' parts inventory system used in manufacturing for 20 years.

Feed the Cash Cows and Starve the Hogs

Being in a turnaround situation isn't necessarily a time of desperation. It is a time of change because what worked previously no longer works, or isn't working as well as you want. Either things have changed and your business needs to adjust, or you're just not satisfied with the level of performance you're achieving right now. Any of these factors can necessitate a change of direction for the business.

> **"In order to grow, it often pays to say 'no.'"**

My experience working with businesses in a turnaround situation indicates that while most business leaders automatically assume that they are suddenly in survival mode – and many are – the mistake they make is to THINK like they are in survival mode. They think day-to-day and short-term. They live from hand to mouth.

Now while this may in fact be their reality, thinking and behaving in this way is severely limiting. Instead, they should look at different horizons. They need to look ahead and begin thinking that way.

So what is a cash cow, you ask?

If you have something that, when you put a dollar in, you soon get dollars out, that is a cash cow. You get results predictably, reliably and consistently. Invest today and reap a benefit tomorrow.

But cash cows do not just involve commodities or other tangibles. Clients can be cash cows, too, because they can also generate increased revenue for your business. You can also grow a client until impressive revenues are generated. But here you do need to keep in mind the cost to service your clients. Are they all worth it or are some just not worth the cost? It may cost you more in service costs than you stand to reap in some situations.

My experience working with businesses also shows that in order to grow, it often pays to say "no." Some clients really are more trouble (to your bottom line) than they are worth and you could be better off getting rid of them. If a relationship with your client no longer works for you, help them to find another supplier who would be happy to service them. That way you will keep your relationship with them in good shape and you will have solved a profitability issue at the same time.

This happened for me in the shop-fitting/signage manufacturing company I started. I had built it up to 55 employees and over $12 million a year in turnover; however, the clients that helped me get started in the end were costing me money to keep. Our overheads had grown with our expansion so therefore the old prices that my original customers were used to paying were no longer sustainable. And by doing these smaller jobs it cost us from an opportunity point of view as it meant we were missing out on much larger and high profit work. The company had gone from doing the small retail single store work to major multi-million dollar fit outs for companies such as Toys R Us and the Walt Disney Company.

I remember it was an emotionally difficult decision to say no to the very people who had helped me get to where I currently was but it was a case of have to, to ensure the ongoing success of a now much larger corporation. This will eventually happen as you grow and expand.

You have to constantly ask yourself this question: Is the light you get worth the candle you burn? Understand that some people are a faucet while others are a drain. It's just the way it is.

DAY 8: Action Checklist

Welcome to the homestretch. In business turnarounds, like in horse-racing, the home-stretch often determines the final results. It's the place where positions can change and strategies sometimes switched that sometimes make all the difference. Most of all you have to recognize what's working and change what's not. This isn't time to change "horses" but it is the time to leverage your strengths and make the maximum impact in your thinking, planning, and upcoming implementation.

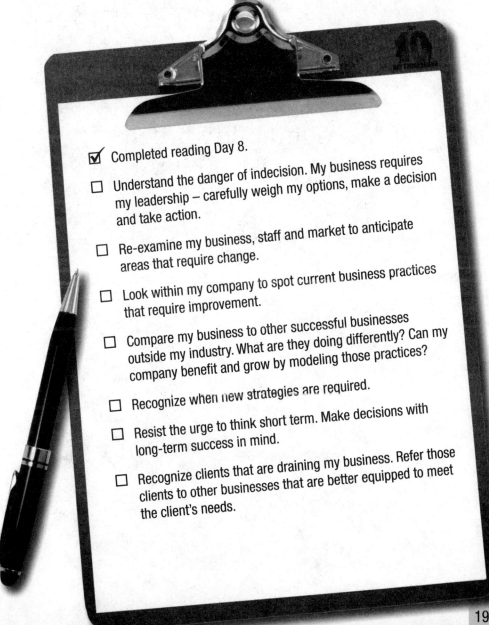

☑ Completed reading Day 8.

☐ Understand the danger of indecision. My business requires my leadership – carefully weigh my options, make a decision and take action.

☐ Re-examine my business, staff and market to anticipate areas that require change.

☐ Look within my company to spot current business practices that require improvement.

☐ Compare my business to other successful businesses outside my industry. What are they doing differently? Can my company benefit and grow by modeling those practices?

☐ Recognize when new strategies are required.

☐ Resist the urge to think short term. Make decisions with long-term success in mind.

☐ Recognize clients that are draining my business. Refer those clients to other businesses that are better equipped to meet the client's needs.

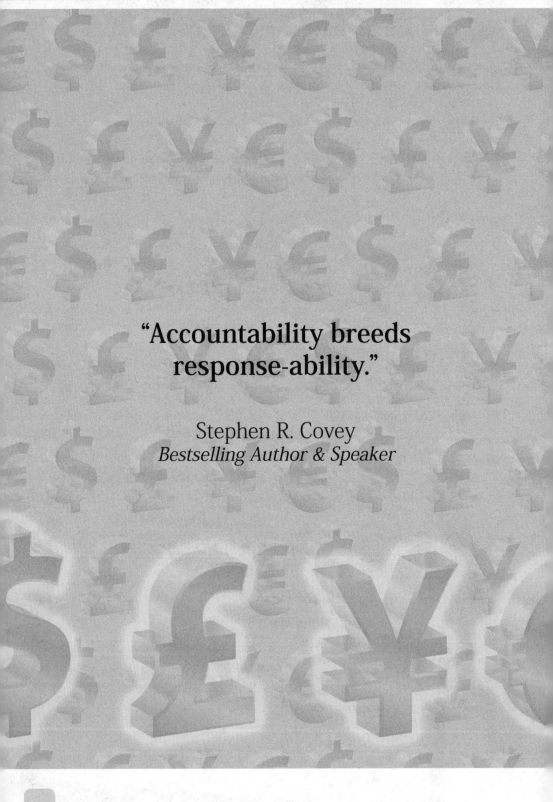

"Accountability breeds
response-ability."

Stephen R. Covey
Bestselling Author & Speaker

Chapter 9

Day 9

The
10
DAY TURNAROUND

Creating Accountability

Chapter 9
Creating Accountability

Nearly there. Today and tomorrow are critical days... the final days in the 10 Day Turnaround. So let's get right to it!

Leadership and management would have to be the most misunderstood concepts in business today. Confusion here is going to have a detrimental effect on your team. Misunderstandings and discontent are sure to follow.

Lead People and Manage Activities

Vince Lombardi said, "Leaders aren't born, they are made. And they are made just like anything else, through hard work."

> **"Leadership and management are two very different concepts."**

Leadership and management are two very different concepts; being a leader may involve managing but it doesn't have to. Similarly, not all managers are leaders.

Let's now look at these two functions in more detail because if you are going to turn your business around successfully, you are going to need a thorough grasp of these two vitally important concepts.

A leader is a guiding or directing head. A leader shows the way. According to the dictionary, to lead is also to influence or induce.

A manager, on the other hand, is someone charged with the management or direction of an organization. To manage is to handle, direct, govern or control in action or use.

Did you spot the subtle difference between the two? Basically leaders inspire and managers manage.

What commonly happens in business today is that many managers, leaders and business owners try to manage their people by giving them an assignment or responsibilities and then tell them how to do those things they are responsible for.

One of the key things you, as a manager or leader, need to be very clear about, especially in a turnaround situation, is to be very precise about the direction you give your people; you must be very consistent in getting a buy-in or commitment from the people who are around you. In this way you will lead them in a manner that allows them to have an opportunity to succeed or fail based on their own skills, knowledge and commitments. Now you are able to hold them accountable for the results they need to achieve, provided that you give them the resources necessary to achieve success.

When you place blame, you surrender your power. Never ask anyone to do something that serves your values without giving them a reason and a way to serve their own at the same time.

I have found that good leaders are motivated by long-term vision and directed by immediate priorities. For them the future creates the present.

"Leverage the talent, time and energy of other people by engaging them in your vision."

Leverage the talent, time and energy of other people by engaging them in your vision— for their reasons, not yours. Do only what you do best and better than anyone else around you. And remember to delegate functions, not tasks.

Some years ago a leading American businessman gave me some wonderful advice. He said to hire slowly and fire fast. The more I thought about that, the more sense it made and it has lived with me ever since.

"Hire slowly and fire fast."

Aspire to Greatness and Inspire a New Reality

One of the key lessons I have learned working with businesses in a turnaround situation over the years is that you can't simply aspire to survive. I would like to emphasize again that a turnaround situation doesn't necessarily mean a point of desperation. It could simply mean that you want to turn around from where you are at now to a higher level of performance because that performance isn't meeting your expectations. Your business could, at this point, still be very successful and profitable.

"Always be aiming to aspire to greatness."

I would like to reiterate that you should always be aiming to aspire to greatness because if you aspire to mediocrity, that's all you will ever be; you will at best be below average.

But if you aspire to greatness, it will ensure you are always setting the bar a little higher, and it will ensure that you will be aspiring towards the things you are really good at rather than the things anyone can do.

By raising the bar and pushing for something greater than what you are achieving at present, you will be inspiring a new reality for your business and all those who work in it.

During the turnaround situation, when something significant needs to change, you want to inspire the people around you (whether they be your team, your clients, your marketplace or even in some cases your competition) to the realization that the way things are at present needn't be the way it has to be. You want to inspire them to understand that the way things have always been isn't necessarily the way it needs to be going forward.
The new reality has to be that there is a possibility that something has got to change. Now your role as a leader has to be to get them to understand that this isn't going to be a 'dictated' change but rather a collaborative change that isn't just for your reasons but for theirs as well.

Another good reason to aspire to greatness has to do with the fact that we, as humans, tend to aim higher than the results we get. When I was young, my mother always used to tell me at the dinner table that my eyes were bigger than my stomach. It's the same with life in general. If you do a good job, you tend to get poor returns, but if you do a great job, you get good returns. However if you do an outstanding job, you will invariably get great returns. This is why you need to aspire to real greatness at all times, and not just for what is acceptable.

> "By aiming beyond the barrier it allows you to break through the barrier."

The world is full of examples that back this up. Take martial arts, as an example. Have you ever seen a black belt attempting to break a board with his fist? He punches *through* the target, not *at* it. By aiming beyond the barrier, it allows you to break through the barrier.

Create a Culture of Accountability

Creating a culture of accountability is fundamental to any form of change. This is true whether it is for personal change, individual change, professional change or organizational change. Whatever you commit to, you have to be held accountable for achieving it.

Whether you are the owner of the business, a leader in the business or even you hold yourself accountable or have an accountability partner or coach, accountability comes from the following:

1. Having a very clear sense of direction
2. Having a very clear assessment of what's possible in terms of the individuals and the organization
3. Having a solid course of action in terms of what you think is necessary in order for the desired results to be achieved
4. Having a mutual commitment from all the people involved in the process to making it happen

Once you have commitment to the process, then everyone is accountable to that process and every individual is accountable for their role and contribution in making that change occur. Admire loyalty; appreciate effort... but reward results.

I have found that one of the things that tend to happen in business, especially when they get into trouble, is that they overlook the small flaws in people's performance and in some cases they won't even address them. They will virtually ignore the performance gaps that someone in the organization has. Not only is this ineffective, it's not fair. If someone isn't aware that what they are doing isn't effective or is problematic, then they don't have the opportunity to change in accordance with what management expects of them.

The worst thing you can do is to not give a team member the opportunity to change and then hold them accountable after the fact. You have to be able to hold them accountable only to the commitments that have been made.

As a leader, you should admire, compliment and recognize efforts people make because sometimes results take time to achieve. Don't make the mistake of recognizing only results.

You need to make sure you reinforce your team on a positive basis. Forget negative reinforcement; it simply doesn't work. It may be your inclination but remember, as members of the animal kingdom, we respond best to positive reinforcement. Just think of how they train dogs, dolphins and even wild animals like lions and elephants to do tricks and you will know what I mean.

Remember that ultimately people get rewarded for performance and results and if you reward their efforts but not their results, you will end up with a bunch of well paid people who aren't getting anything done.

Over the years surveys into the attributes of high performing businesses have shown that there are six key things those businesses all had in common. They are:

1. A high performance challenge
2. A bias for excellence
3. A bias for solutions
4. A bias for urgency
5. A bias for self-monitoring
6. A bias for transparency

In a turnaround situation, you need to have a clear sense of direction as well as what you are trying to accomplish, you need a pretty good understanding of what your expectations are and you need mutual buy-in from all concerned.

From this starting point, people have to have a willingness to achieve, be it an intrinsic reward or measuring system that says, 'I really and truly want to do this'. There has to be some form of motivation with a performance reward system in place.

You Get To Eat What You Kill

As a turnaround leader or manager you really want to be able to compensate people based on the things they have influence (and hopefully control) over at the very least, and their ability to achieve and accomplish.

As an illustration of this, I am reminded of the time I was consulting for a fairly large company who were in the midst of turning around. One of the senior managers came into my office after everyone had committed to doing whatever it took to achieve change, and said, "What I really need from you is a guarantee."

I responded by saying, "I've got to tell you that at present, I am about $200,000 short for the payroll at the end of the month and we're behind on paying just about every vendor in sight. So I am going to give you the same guarantee that I am giving everyone else. I am going to give you two weeks, and at the end of that time, if you have either generated more money than it costs to keep you or you have saved the company more money than it costs to pay you, I'll give you another two weeks. That's my guarantee."

I then went on to explain that at the end of the two weeks, if he couldn't demonstrate that he had made or saved the company money that was equal to or greater than that which it cost to keep him, he would be gone.

It might sound harsh but at the time I hadn't taken a penny in salary for months and several other executives hadn't taken pay checks for weeks.

This manager really needed to know that, because the bottom line was that the company was going out of business if we weren't able to turn the business around in a hurry. There was literally nothing that could be guaranteed other than the opportunity to turn the company around.

To Measure is to Know

One of the basic concepts of running a successful business is to measure everything. I live by the rule that what gets measured can be controlled and what gets measured gets done.

> "What gets measured gets done."

I have generally found that in most businesses, what gets done compared to what is planned to get done is around 50% at best when there is no form of measuring or monitoring taking place.

This is where the powerful concept of key performance indicators comes in.

KPIs and ROI

When people know that something is being measured, and it doesn't matter if it's their activities, their results or their on-going efforts, then they will know very clearly what success looks like for them. If they don't have some form of measurement of what success looks like, it becomes very difficult for them to achieve it. It also becomes almost impossible for people to have a consensus on it. This, of course, is disastrous, especially for companies in the turnaround situation.

I remember a person applying for a general manger position with one of my companies. In the interview I asked him why he left his last general manger position. He answered, "I couldn't achieve the success I was looking for at that company." So I asked him what success looked like to him.

He looked puzzled by my question and I watched him as his eyes searched from side-to-side while searching for a response. He then replied, "I'm not really sure, but I just know that I didn't achieve it at the last company". Yet again I continued with my questioning. This time I asked him, "Well, if you don't know what success actually looks like to you, how do you know that you didn't already achieve it at the last company?"

There was silence as the penny dropped. Needless to say, I finished up the interview and didn't employ him. The lesson here is he couldn't define what success was to him so it stood to reason that he wouldn't find it working with me either. Then I would have wasted my time training and employing someone who would have eventually left us for the same reason ...he wasn't achieving the success he wanted!

Make sure you can clearly define what it is you want and what that looks, sounds and feels like when you have it.

If you can measure it, there is a good chance it can get done.

The same applies to your return on investment. If you invest a dollar, you need to know when you will be able to get it back, with interest. For example, if you knew that for every dollar you invested in your business, you would get twice as much back in three years time, you might not be in a position to wait that long for your return on investment.

Unless you can measure these variables, you wouldn't know whether they were working in your favor or not. You certainly wouldn't know whether your efforts, and those of your people, were paying off and moving you closer to your objectives or not.

Measurement is one of the keys to a successful turnaround.

Hire Slowly and Fire Fast

This is particularly important, especially in a turnaround situation. If you are hiring people and asking them to do something that may be a little unusual and outside the norm, you need to give your team some say or buy-in as to who is coming into the organization.

Make sure you are not the only one making the hiring decisions. This is important because if people are going to be mutually affected and have an interdependency regarding their survival, their success or their significance as an organization, in many cases it is beneficial to have other perspectives.

There are many effective tools you could use to assist with the decision-making process here. For instance, you may want to use the DISC Profile test. This is a system that has been used around the world since 1928 to conduct personality behavioral profiling of candidates, usually to improve lives, interpersonal relationships, work productivity, teamwork and communication.

OUTGOING

T A S K

D I
S C

P E O P L E

RESERVED

D = Dominance - Determined, Driver, A Doer
Impatient/Anger

I = Influencer - Inspiring, Involved, Interacting
Optimistic

S = Steady - Supportive, Status Quo, Stable
Unexpressive

C = Compliant - Cautious, Conscientious, Calculating
Fearful

---

* Reference www.The10dayTurnaround.com/Disc-profile-Reference

Behavioral research suggests that the most effective people are those who understand themselves, both their strengths and weaknesses, so they can develop strategies to meet the demands of their environment.

A person's behavior is a necessary and integral part of who they are. In other words, much of our behavior comes from "nature" (inherent), and much comes from "nurture" (our upbringing). It is the universal language of "how we act," or our observable human behavior.

DISC is an OBSERVABLE LANGUAGE – we can see how people behave.

A UNIVERSAL LANGUAGE – it doesn't matter what culture a person is from.

A NEUTRAL LANGUAGE – there is no right or wrong behavioral style.

A SILENT LANGUAGE – knowledge of DISC behavior is not used to manipulate people.

Read through the different styles and see if you can identify yourself, or a member of your team. To help you have a better understanding we have given as examples of some well-known people and the behavioral style displayed.

D Style – Donald Trump, for example displays typical "D" characteristics such as he's dominate, decisive, direct, results – oriented, challenge – oriented he's innovative and persistent.

I Style – Former President Bill Clinton and Richard Branson for example display "I" characteristics such as they're charming, confident, convincing, enthusiastic, inspiring, optimistic and persuasive.

S Style – Forest Gump (played by actor Tom Hanks) for example displays typical "S" characteristics such as he's friendly, a good listener, patient, relaxed, sincere, steady and a team player.

C Style – Warren Buffett and Bill Gates for example display "C" characteristics such as they're analytical, accurate, conscientious and steady, diplomatic, fact finders and have high standards.

D BEHAVIORAL STYLE

DESCRIPTORS	<ul><li>Adventuresome</li><li>Competitive</li><li>Daring</li><li>Decisive</li><li>Direct</li><li>Innovative</li><li>Persistent</li><li>Problem Solver</li><li>Results-oriented</li><li>Self-starter</li></ul>
VALUE TO THE TEAM	<ul><li>Bottom line organizer</li><li>Forward-looking</li><li>Challenge-oriented</li><li>Initiates activity</li><li>Innovative</li></ul>
IDEAL ENVIRONMENT	<ul><li>An innovative and futuristic-oriented environment</li><li>Forum to express ideas and viewpoints</li><li>Non-routine work</li><li>Work with challenge and opportunity</li></ul>
TENDENCY UNDER STRESS	<ul><li>Demanding</li><li>Nervy</li><li>Aggressive</li><li>Egotistical</li></ul>
POSSIBLE LIMITATIONS	<ul><li>Overuse of position</li><li>Set standards too high</li><li>Lack tact and diplomacy</li><li>Take on too much, too soon, too fast</li></ul>EMOTION OF THE HIGH D: Anger

I BEHAVIORAL STYLE

DESCRIPTORS	<ul><li>Charming</li><li>Confident</li><li>Convincing</li><li>Enthusiastic</li><li>Inspiring</li><li>Optimistic</li><li>Persuasive</li><li>Popular</li><li>Sociable</li><li>Trusting</li></ul>
VALUE TO THE TEAM	<ul><li>Optimism and enthusiasm</li><li>Creative problem solving</li><li>Motivates others toward goals</li><li>Team player</li><li>Negotiates conflicts</li></ul>
IDEAL ENVIRONMENT	<ul><li>High degree of people contact</li><li>Freedom from control and detail</li><li>Freedom from movement</li><li>Forum for ideas to be heard</li><li>Democratic supervisor with whom he can associate</li></ul>
TENDENCY UNDER STRESS	<ul><li>Self-promoting</li><li>Overly optimistic</li><li>Gabby</li><li>Unrealistic</li></ul>
POSSIBLE LIMITATIONS	<ul><li>Inattentive to details</li><li>Be unrealistic in appraising people</li><li>Trust people indiscriminately</li><li>Situational listener</li></ul> EMOTION OF THE HIGH I: Optimism

S BEHAVIORAL STYLE

DESCRIPTORS	<ul><li>Amiable</li><li>Friendly</li><li>Good listener</li><li>Patient</li><li>Relaxed</li><li>Sincere</li><li>Stable</li><li>Steady</li><li>Team Player</li><li>Understanding</li></ul>
VALUE TO THE TEAM	<ul><li>Dependable team player</li><li>Work for a leader and a cause</li><li>Patient and empathetic</li><li>Logical step-wise thinker</li><li>Service-oriented</li></ul>
IDEAL ENVIRONMENT	<ul><li>Stable and predictable environment</li><li>Environment that allows time to change</li><li>Long-term work relationships</li><li>Little conflict between people</li><li>Freedom from restrictive rules</li></ul>
TENDENCY UNDER STRESS	<ul><li>Non-demonstrative</li><li>Unconcerned</li><li>Hesitant</li><li>Inflexible</li></ul>
POSSIBLE LIMITATIONS	<ul><li>Yield to avoid controversy</li><li>Difficulty in establishing priorities</li><li>Dislike of unwarranted change</li><li>Difficulty dealing with diverse situations</li></ul> EMOTION OF THE HIGH S: Non-emotional

C BEHAVIORAL STYLE	
DESCRIPTORS	<ul><li>Accurate</li><li>Analytical</li><li>Conscientious</li><li>Courteous</li><li>Diplomatic</li><li>Fact-finder</li><li>High Standards</li><li>Mature</li><li>Patient</li><li>Precise</li></ul>
VALUE TO THE TEAM	<ul><li>Maintains high standards</li><li>Conscientious and steady</li><li>Defines, clarifies, gets information and tests</li><li>Objective – "The anchor of reality"</li><li>Comprehensive problem solver</li></ul>
IDEAL ENVIRONMENT	<ul><li>Where critical thinking is needed</li><li>Technical work or specialized area</li><li>Close relationship with small group</li><li>Familiar work environment</li><li>Private office or work area</li></ul>
TENDENCY UNDER STRESS	<ul><li>Pessimistic</li><li>Picky</li><li>Fussy</li><li>Overly critical</li></ul>
POSSIBLE LIMITATIONS	<ul><li>Be defensive when criticized</li><li>Get bogged down in details</li><li>Be overly intense for the situation</li><li>Appear somewhat aloof and cool</li></ul> EMOTION OF THE HIGH C: Fear

KEYS TO ADAPTING COMMUNICATION

D COMMUNICATING WITH THE HIGH D

- Be clear, specific and to the point.
  Don't ramble on, or waste their time.
- Stick to business.
  Don't try to build personal relationships, or chitchat.
- Come prepared wit all requirements, objectives and support material in a well-organized package.
  Don't forget or lose things, be unprepared or disorganized.
- Present the facts logically; plan your presentation efficiently.
  Don't leave loopholes or cloudy issues if you don't want to be zapped!
- Ask specific (preferably What?) questions.
  Don't ask rhetorical questions,or useless ones.
- Provide alternatives and choices for making decisions.
  Don't come up with decisions made, or make it for them.
- Provide facts and figures about probability of success or the effectiveness of options.
  Don't speculate wildly or offer guarantees and assurances where there is a risk in meeting them.
- If you disagree, take issue with the facts.
  Don't take issue with the High D personally.
- Provide win/win opportunity.
  Don't force a High D into a losing situation.

I COMMUNICATING WITH THE HIGH I

- Plan interaction that supports their dreams and intentions.
  Don't legislate or muffle.
- Allow time for relating and socializing.
  Don't be curt, cold or tight-lipped.
- Talk to people about their goals.
  Don't drive to facts, figures and alternatives.
- Focus on people and action items. Put details in writing
  Don't leave decisions up in the air.
- As for their opinion.
  Don't be impersonal or task-oriented.
- Provide ideas for implementing action.
  Don't waste time in"dreaming".
- Use enough time to be stimulating, fun, fast moving.
  Don't cut the meeting short or be too business-like.
- Provide testimonials from people they see as important or prominent.
  Don't talk down to them.
- Offer special, immediate and extra incentives for their willingness to take risks.
  Don't take too much time. Get to action items.

S COMMUNICATING WITH THE HIGH S

- Start with personal comments. Break the ice.
  Don't rush headlong into business or the agenda.
- Show sincere interest in them as people.
  Don't stick coldly or harshly to business.
- Patiently draw out their personal goals and ideas. Listen and be responsive.
  Don't force a quick response to your objectives.
- Present your case logically, softly, non-threateningly.
  Don't threaten with positional power or be demanding.
- Ask specific (preferably How?) questions.
  Don't interrupt as they speak. Listen carefully.
- Move casually, informally.
  Don't be abrupt and rapid.
- If you disagree, prove it with data, facts or testimonials from respected people.
  Don't mistake their willingness to go along for satisfaction.
- Provide personal assurances and guarantees.
  Don't promise something you can't deliver.
- If a decision is required of them, allow them time to think.
  Don't force a quick decision, provide information.

C COMMUNICATING WITH THE HIGH C

- Prepare your case in advance.
  Don't be disorganized or messy.
- Approach them in a straightforward, direct way.
  Don't be casual, informal or personal.
- Use a thoughtful approach. Build credibility by looking at all sides of each issue.
  Don't force a quick decision.
- Present specifics and do what you say you can do.
  Don't be vague about expectations or fail to follow through.
- Draw up an "Action Plan" with scheduled dates and milestones.
  Don't over promise as to results, be conservative.
- Take your time, but be persistent.
  Don't be abrupt and rapid.
- If you disagree, prove it with data, facts or testimonials from respected people.
  Don't appeal to opinion or feelings as evidence.
- Provide them with the information and the time they need to make a decision.
  Don't use closes, use incentives to get the decision.
- Allow them their space.
  Don't touch them.

For more information and a sample of DISC Personality styles and how to communicate or even sell to the different styles, visit the resource page at the 10 Day Turnaround website. www.the10dayturnaround.com/resources.

As a business leader in a turnaround situation, you want to be able to make good decisions about who you are hiring, why you are hiring them, what's expected of them and what the performance measures are so that they know what success looks like.

The new team player really needs to have a good understanding too of what's possible and what's not.

Furthermore, as the leader, if a team member is not meeting their obligations, you need to make them aware of it, you need to be able to help them correct it and if they can't or won't, the bottom line is they shouldn't remain in the organization.

This raises an interesting point. It's the difference between can't and won't. This reminds me of what I call the Rambo Test. You may not want to do something silly like sing at the top of your voice in a quiet library, but if someone were to offer you $100,000 to do so, you might sing without thinking twice about it. This demonstrates the difference between can't and won't. You see if after being offered $100,000 you still don't, chances are you can't.

Let me give you another example. When I was still growing up, my mother once told me to do something simple, like tying my shoes. I forget the exact task but I remember the lesson. She asked me to do it and I said I couldn't. I can still hear her saying that when I said I couldn't, I was actually telling her one of two things: either I didn't know how, in which case she was going to teach me, or I was telling her that I wouldn't, in which case she was going to beat me. She then wanted to know which one it was—couldn't or wouldn't.

What this points out to us as business leaders is that when someone doesn't have the ability to do something, you may be able to subsidize, train or develop them so that they can meet their commitments.

But it may be that they just won't, in which case you simply can't afford to keep them.

Once I hired the wrong person and it cost me $250,000. Had I known the DISC profile of that person, I would never have hired him simply because he wasn't suited for the role he was in. The job was as an estimator, yet his attention to detail was virtually zero. This person was a real extrovert, very friendly and outgoing and left out a whole lot of calculations on how many screws would be used for an international shop fitting project. His Behavioral Style was an "I" and what I should have had for a person in this position was a Behavioral style of a "C".

My mistake here was I hired him on personality and not on the unconscious mind skill set that was needed for him to be really effective in that position.

Remember, hire people for their skills for the position, which sometimes means that person may have a totally different personality than you. My wife is a great example of that. She loves spending time working out financial formulas and figures, accounting and problem solving with numbers. However for me, that would simply drive me crazy and I would find it a real chore. Yet for her it's hugely pleasurable.

DAY 9: Action Checklist

Gut check time - time to hold yourself (and others) accountable for results. Have you completed all of the assignments and activities so far in this book? While we like to be tender-hearted now is time for a bit of tough love. If you've done your best thus far, it's certainly reasonable to expect and inspire the best in others. If you haven't perhaps it's time to go back and hold yourself accountable to your dreams, desires and commitments. Once you've completed all the assignments in the book necessary for your success, complete the checklist below.

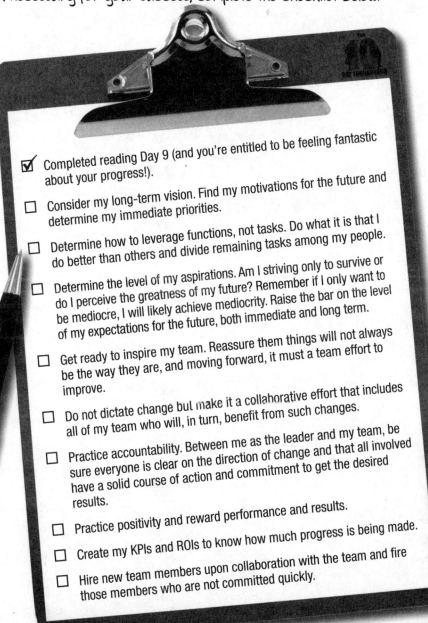

☑ Completed reading Day 9 (and you're entitled to be feeling fantastic about your progress!).

☐ Consider my long-term vision. Find my motivations for the future and determine my immediate priorities.

☐ Determine how to leverage functions, not tasks. Do what it is that I do better than others and divide remaining tasks among my people.

☐ Determine the level of my aspirations. Am I striving only to survive or do I perceive the greatness of my future? Remember if I only want to be mediocre, I will likely achieve mediocrity. Raise the bar on the level of my expectations for the future, both immediate and long term.

☐ Get ready to inspire my team. Reassure them things will not always be the way they are, and moving forward, it must a team effort to improve.

☐ Do not dictate change but make it a collaborative effort that includes all of my team who will, in turn, benefit from such changes.

☐ Practice accountability. Between me as the leader and my team, be sure everyone is clear on the direction of change and that all involved have a solid course of action and commitment to get the desired results.

☐ Practice positivity and reward performance and results.

☐ Create my KPIs and ROIs to know how much progress is being made.

☐ Hire new team members upon collaboration with the team and fire those members who are not committed quickly.

"You cannot escape the
responsibility of tomorrow
by evading it today."

Abraham Lincoln

Chapter 10

Day 10

Creating Instant Wins

Chapter 10
Creating Instant Wins

You've done it – you've created a new way to think about your business, to act, to lead, and to develop accountability. What you've accomplished in such a short amount of time, *while still running your business*, is truly awesome.

We're almost at the end of the journey!

So let's get right to it...

When in a turnaround situation, it is important to look at things from different horizons; ones that may not necessarily be the most strategic or offer the most impact over time.

Create Immediate 'Wins'

Look for things that you can make immediate progress on. Look for things that you can implement today that will give you a payback tomorrow. This is important because one of the things you will want to achieve at this point is building the confidence of your team in your turnaround plan and that it is working.

Unsettling times call for tough action but they also call for understanding, sensitivity and thoughtfulness. Turning around a business successfully demands commitment from the entire team; it depends on the buy-in of everyone involved with the business.

Wins measure the effectiveness of everyone's actions. It's like keeping score. People use wins as a gauge of their efforts and a measure of their success.

Time and Priorities

There is no such thing as time management—can't be done. Don't believe me, try telling time to stop. Try speeding it up—you can't control time; you can only control your actions and manage your priorities.

First things first, next things next, last things last. Easy to say, harder to do, even hard to stay consistently disciplined in turnaround times.

How do you know where to start? What tells you what to do first, second, third—today, tomorrow, and for the foreseeable future?

Quite simply, you start, continue, and end with what will have the greatest, most immediate impact on your business, in the shortest time possible with the greatest amount of ease.

Each and every evaluation of your business begins with questioning what is and assessing what could be. In every possibility, there are a number of factors that are key – relevancy and probability.

Relevancy is measured in terms of the strategic and tactical impact on your business and your turnaround plan. Probability is best evaluated in terms of your resources (what's needed and available or accessible), and the time and energy necessary to turn a "possibility" into a "reality".

Remember the Pareto Principle or the 80/20 rule? In most every area of life, business, or society roughly 80% of the effects are the result of some 20% of the causes. Choose well, your success is almost certain, choose wrong and it's a formula for frustration at best and a fast path to extinction.

Over the years, we've developed, used, and been exposed to just about every priority-setting, decision-making system, tool, and turnaround technology out there. Our goal throughout the book is not to clutter your mind or try to bedazzle you with complexity. Simplicity over sophistication; effectiveness over erudition is a motto and a mode of operation.

By now through reading this book, you've thought of, imagined, considered, and created dozens of possibilities for improving your business—for doing things better, faster, cheaper, more effectively and efficiently. You've evaluated the people and the activities in your business. You've thought deeply about your product or service, your market, and your business model. Now is the time for not only "action" but "right action".

Start by making a list of all of the strategic and tactical changes you would like or need to make in your business. Write a brief explanation of the change but leave plenty of blank space between each "change-factor". Think about each "change-factor" in terms of the importance or impact the successful implementation would have on your business on a scale of zero-to-ten, with "ten" being of the highest importance and impact. Write the corresponding number beside each "change".

Next, underneath each "change-factor" item on your list, note the key actions or steps required to implement the change. What resources will be required and which resources that are needed do you currently have or have access to? How long will it take to complete each step and how long will it be before the impact will be realized on your business? How easy or difficult will it be to implement? What is the degree of probability or certainty that the "change-factor" can be and will be implemented in the time frame you expect? Again, rate each change-factor on a scale of "zero-to-ten".

Review your list of change factors that have the highest score on both the "Importance/Impact" and the "Time/Ease" scales.

Rarely if ever, are there many, if any, "change-factors" that score "tens" on both axes; if they exist, they've usually been started, implemented, or completed. What you're looking for are change elements that score highly on both axes, "the 20%" so to speak. The change elements that score "seven" or above in both criteria elements or perhaps a "ten" in one element and perhaps a "six" in the other criteria.

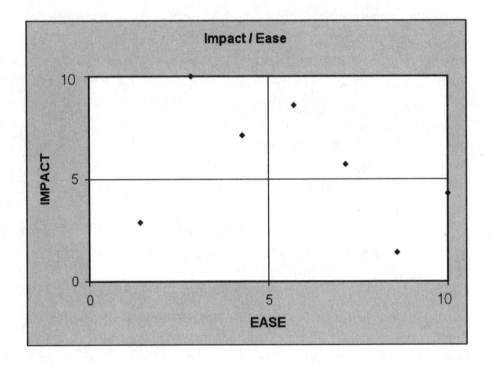

Let me illustrate it for you.

(Note to reader: If you'd like to explore our proprietary Impact/ Ease Grid software you can do so at: www.the10dayturnaround. com).

Reallocate Your Resources

In some cases, you may have to reallocate your resources. If, for instance, you have been operating very strategically in terms of your business model but this turns out to be the wrong business model or strategy, you may be doing the right things within the context of that model or strategy, but they may not necessarily be the right things for your business in terms of the environment that you are operating in.

This may mean you need to reallocate your resources; this could be your attention, your people, your capital, your physical assets, or anything that goes into operating your business model.

Now here's the important thing: this reallocation of resources must be based on a time horizon that allows you to get immediate wins and have an immediate impact.

Simplify and Optimize

One of the ways to help you achieve immediate wins is to have a good look at the inner operational systems used in your business because overcoming any inherent bottlenecks or impediments can unlock pent-up results quickly.

You may, for instance, have a very complicated sales system, an overly complex marketing system or a complex strategy in terms of how you go about growing your business. In cases like this, you need to simplify things.

You need to investigate what you can do to get more out of the market you are currently operating in instead of going out, like many do, and developing a brand new market.

What can you do to get your current clients to buy more often? Or perhaps you can get them to buy faster or to buy different things from you. Perhaps you can achieve this by putting together a joint venture or adding new products or services to your product line-up.

There are a lot of effective things that can be done to grow your business fast through simplifying and optimizing the resources that you currently have on board. These fall into five basic categories and are summarized in the table below.

5 Levers of Strategic Profit Growth

| No. of Leads/ Prospects | X | Conversion Rate | = | No. of Customers | X | No. of Transactions | X | Average $$$ Sale | = | Turnover | X | Margins | = | Profits |

Lead Generation		Conversion Rate		Number of Transactions		Increasing Size of the Sale		Increase Profits
1. Company Website	1. Define Your Ideal Prospect	1. Communicate Frequently	1. Increase Your Prices	1. Increase Your Prices
2. Web Banner Ads	2. Develop Your Unique Value	2. Run Special Promotions	2. Up Sell/Down-Sell	2. Introduce Performance-based Pay
3. Article Marketing	3. Create a Benefits List	3. Offer Frequency Incentives	3. Cross or Add On Sell	3. Outsource/Use Virtual Employees
4. Blog Postin	4. Offer a Guarantee/Risk Reversal	4. Create a Loyalty Program	4. Create Product Bundles	4. "Lease" or "Own" Expertise
5. Newspaper Advertising	5. Offer Payment Terms/ Discounts	5. Develop/Source New Products	5. Offer Bulk Pricing/ Packaging	5. Use Barter
6. Classified Ads	6. Utilize Urgency Incentives	6. Use Planned Product Obsolescence	6. Introduce Higher Priced Products	6. Conduct a Cost and Activity Audit
7. Television Advertising	7. Use Limited Time/Qty. Offers	7. Create a Culture of Innovation	7. Introduce Add-on Warranties	7. Improve Quality
8. Radio Advertising	8. Add New Forms of Payment	8. Enhance Your Customer Service	8. Consider Minimum Order Sizing	8. Eliminate Waste/Recycle
9. Magazine Advertising	9. Develop Standardize Sales Scripts	9. Use Outbound Sales Calling	9. Stock More High Priced Ranges	9. Reduce Redundancy
10. Trade Journal Advertising	10. Learn Consultative Selling	10. Introduce Up-selling	10. Create a Quality Image	10. Sell Via Party Plan/ Multi Level
11. Industry Newsletter Ads	11. Measure Your Sales Activities	11. Offer Seasonal Incentives	11. Eliminate Selling Discounts	11. Commission Only Sales Team
12. Newsletters	12. Create Referral Programs	12. Offer Free Trials of New Products	12. Point of Sale Material	12. Provide Team Training
13. Mail Inserts	13. Set up a Follow-up Program	13. Use Joint Venture Selling	13. Impulse Buys	13. Pay NO Overtime
14. Public Relations	14. Conduct Needs Analyses	14. Leverage a CRM System	14. Product Packaging	14. Reduce Team Size
	Client Surveys		15. Sell with an Either/Or Question	15. Reduce Unnecessary Managers

For a comprehensive version of this chart go to www.The10DayTurnaround.com/resources.

The other area to work on at this point is optimization. We have already touched on this earlier when we spoke about thinking inside and outside the box, but there are other ways to optimize and you need to focus on these now.

You may need to develop ways to become more efficient in terms of your management systems and structures and the decision-making process. You may need to think about optimizing your sales force in terms of having them working with the right prospects and the right sales presentations.

You may be able to optimize your cash by moving it into an interest-bearing account.

Stimulate and Innovate

If you can get someone to do something now that would normally take them six months to get around to doing, or if you could stimulate an activity that makes it occur now, that is the way to go, especially during a turnaround situation.

You want to be doing whatever you can to stimulate performance, desire, motivation, change and more effectiveness in your process.

It has always amazed me that so many business leaders are of the view that when it comes to innovation, they immediately assume they must think in terms of technology. Now this is probably due to the great job our technological innovators have done over the years by changing our lives through their ideas. But from a business point-of-view this is a severely limited way of thinking. It probably accounts for the lack of innovation in general in the small business community.

Innovation involves doing something in a new or unique way that hasn't been done (or has been done inconsistently) previously. I'm not talking about things that are big, grand or earth-shattering, but anything that is different and effective.

The Optimization Mirror and The Innovation Window

A final comment on optimization and innovation. Generally, the best way to find methods for optimization is to look within your own company and your own industry as if looking in a mirror. The best way to find ideas for innovation is to look outside your company and industry for methods to adapt and adopt to your business as if looking out a window.

Uncover Windfalls

While essentially the same as creating immediate wins, what I'm getting at here is finding ways to get access to new resources. For instance, if a company needs cash, they may have excess inventory that they could liquidate. They may be able to go to a factoring company and factor receivables, or they may have a lot of assets in purchased equipment that they could sell back to a leasing company and then lease the assets back, giving them an immediate influx of cash. They might have past-due receivables that can be sent to a collection agency. There may be payables due that you can negotiate a "full and final payment" agreement.

If you have a building lease, you may be able to consider sub-leasing excess space to another company and this may give you a windfall profit or revenue stream that could allow you to generate cash on a regular basis.

The secret is to look carefully at what you already have and see if there are ways for you to use that differently. I am talking about things that are not currently part of your existing business model.

Every business has untapped assets and hidden opportunities lurking beneath the surface of ordinary thinking. For a list of additional ideas, please visit www.the10dayturnaround.com.

Moving from Struggle to Stability, and then to Success and Beyond

Moving from struggle to stability and beyond is especially critical in a turnaround situation that is driven not by desperation, but by a critical factor like something changing in the economy or the business. In cases like this, you will typically have decided that you need to make the change rather than having to make the change.

In such cases you will find that at some point in time, you have to open your horizons up, especially if you have been taking actions based on short-term needs and priorities.

Let's look at the situation facing a company that is on the point of bankruptcy. They only think about survival and what they need to do to survive the next sixty days. What the businesses leaders soon discover is that unless they look beyond the next sixty days, they will never be able to build a business that can last longer than sixty days.

So at some point in time, you need to open up your horizon in terms of your decision-making, your planning processes and the like so you can go from starving to survival and from there to stability and success. And once you are there, you may want to start thinking about a higher level of success where you can become an industry leader, a community leader or even an innovator.

If you can do this, you will have moved from success to significance.

When most companies are forced into a turnaround, they are almost starving to death. The only thing that you can think about when you are starving is how you can get enough food in your belly, how you can get enough cash, and what you have to do to keep the doors open.

Your aim in a situation like this is to progress from starvation to stability, where you can catch your breath.

Once you become stable you will begin thinking about what you need to do to become successful and then ultimately how to get to a level of significance.

There may be other steps you need to aim for, for instance between survival and stability you may need to aim for scalability, but it all depends on your own particular situation.

Think of the stages as the four or five stages of success. That way you will not only remember them but you will also be able to peg your company on the scale to show where you are at that point in time and what progress you are making.

> "Market when times are good and market some more when times are tough."

Market When Times are Good and Market Some More When Times are Tough

Marketing is not an option – the only option is if it is an investment or an expense.

This is a very important concept to understand as you complete the final day of your turnaround process. You see, it is something that most business owners or leaders do but they do it in reverse. They market vigorously in the good times and cut back on marketing when times get tough.

This is probably an outcome of an accountant's mentality because they tend to look for immediate ways of cutting back when money has to be saved. This is, I believe, due to the way they see the world – through the pages of a ledger.

If you look at a typical ledger, you will see that it is made up of two main sections – a credit section and a debit section. Activities fall into one or other of these two main sections. Call them income and expenditure. Call them pluses and minuses. Whatever you call them, accountants tend to place anything to do with money into one of the two categories. The problem with this approach is that it gives rise to the way of thinking that says marketing is an expense.

Thinking of it as an investment should make it clear that in times of need, the way forward should be to invest rather than to cut back. The way forward is to look for more markets, more customers and more opportunities. It should be obvious that the way to do this is through strategic and effective marketing and not cutting back.

Cutting back is fine for things like discretionary spending and even in some instances wages and similar fixed costs, but marketing ... that's limiting thinking in the extreme. It's like saying a sure way to fix a head cold is to cut your head off. Sure it will fix the cold, but at what cost?

> "The bottom line is if you don't market, you can't sell, and then you can't generate revenue."

The bottom line is if you don't market, you can't sell, and then you can't generate revenue. If you don't generate revenue you can't generate profit, and if you don't generate profit, you go out of business.

As you prepare to communicate change to your team, make sure you know the needs of your marketplace and clients, the benefits of what you provide, and that you have a firm belief in the value of your product, service, your company and yourself.

Marketing is About Communicating Value

What really is marketing? What is the difference between marketing and selling? There is a very clear distinction between the two and it's important you understand exactly what this is as you prepare to describe the 10 Day Turnaround.

How many times have you heard the term 'sales and marketing'? You probably even use it yourself. The problem with this is that for a start, it is backwards. Sales and marketing are not the same thing.

Marketing is all about conveying value to the marketplace. If you convey value to the marketplace, you can obtain interest from the marketplace.

But a sale doesn't occur strictly from marketing. It doesn't occur from only creating a perception of value; it occurs when you also create a perception of trust – when you earn people's trust. You see, what happens is that in order for people to make an investment or spend money, they need trust. If they don't have trust, they simply won't invest or buy.

Marketing is therefore about conveying value and selling is about earning trust. Here is a quick rule of thumb to help you remember the important difference between these two key components:

1. Marketing
    * Gain the attention of the marketplace
    * Convey the value or benefit of your product or service

2. Sales
    * Earn the trust of your prospective buyers
    * Get them to take action

Redefining Your Unique Value Proposition

I prefer not to use the term 'unique selling proposition' but instead 'unique value proposition.' I believe it's not about selling, it's about *creating value*. This term (unique selling proposition or USP for short) originated back in the 1950s and has become, I believe, a little overused.

So on the "morning after" the 10 Day Turnaround, I want you to redefine your unique value proposition. By this I mean understanding what it is that the marketplace wants. Then, in light of this, redefine what's unique about your business, what the benefits are of clients doing business with you (whether it is your product or your service), what problems are being solved, what is it that's being satisfied, what benefits are being gained, what benefits are being realized, and how can you best communicate that to your marketplace, your prospects and your existing clients or customers.

Understand that your existing clients and customers are extremely important because they are the best source of referrals and repeat sales. They are your bread and butter foundation. Be sure that they clearly understand what the values and benefits are in doing business with you as opposed to someone else. They need to know why they should be investing their time, their attention and ultimately their money when they decide they want to enter into a transaction with you.

It's all about being able to clearly understand what that is and convey it clearly too.

Selling Your Way to success

One of the sad facts of life in the business community is that as soon as a business starts to experience difficulties or hardship, they often stop or curtail their marketing activities.

In some cases, they even stop selling! They do this by making it difficult for people to buy.

Let me give you an example: A few years ago I was doing some consulting work for a company, and one of the things they did when business got tight was to limit the number of hours they answered the telephone. I soon found out that people were phoning in after five in the afternoon trying to place orders or to ask questions about orders they had previously placed. These calls were, if they had thought about it carefully, opportunities for them to work with these prospects and customers to make them want to buy, make them want to buy more or to make sales stick.

While they believed they were saving money, what they were actually doing was strangling their sales efforts.

Revenue Comes from Sales And Sales Come from Earning Trust

In many cases you may not have the resources to increase your people's salaries and you may need to cut back on bonuses, but what you can do nevertheless to move them to a higher level of performance is to offer them strong incentives.

This is particularly true when it comes to sales people. You could give them short-term incentives to get sales faster or to go back and reactivate clients who last bought a while ago. There are many creative ways in which you can use sales to generate revenue, and you can then use some of this revenue to create incentives and performance bonuses to further stimulate the people who are going to drive sales.

I remember the time I motivated a local real estate agent to sell my property within 30 days. I had listed my property at a time when the market average selling cycle was between 90 and 120 days. I was concerned as the market was about to turn on a rapid downward spiral due to the subprime loans issues arising in the United States and people losing homes. I knew I had to act fast.

So I motivated the Realtor by offering him a bonus of $2000 above any normal commissions that he would get as a part of the normal sales process. This was conditional that he was to sell my home within 30 days. This worked a treat! He was much more motivated to show more people through my property than any others on the market of a similar standard as he stood to gain $2000 more. And sure enough, he sold our property in 27 days. Then, as I predicted, the market place fell by over $30,000 per property within the next 60 days. So by selling within the 30 days I was effectively $28,000 better off simply by paying out an extra $2000 in commissions. So the moral of the story is: act fast and think outside the square, motivate people to get an expedient result and reward them in the process.

What you should be aiming to do is essentially to sell your way to success.

Make Your Mark and Increase Value

Before you come up with a prescription, you must know a few things about the conditions of your business, your market, and the people who you want to do business with.

Why is it that a potential customer might want to do business with you? Why did your current clients choose to do business with you in the first place? Why did the prospects you lost choose someone else or decide not to buy at all? What was it that caused a once active client to stop buying from you? Why did your current clients decide only to buy what they did, when they did, and how much they did when they bought from you last? What is it that your prospects or clients would just love to buy from YOU that you don't offer or they don't know about? What would it take for a client to buy from you faster, longer or more often? Inquiring minds like ours would like to know and so should you.

Prospects and clients have more choices today than ever before and it's only going to get worse — for the supplier of course.

Years ago, the supplier had the advantage. The business who was looking to sell something knew a prospect had a finite number of choices or options. It could have been because of geography, limited information, limited supply or just plain ignorance of the alternatives that made a prospect buy from a particular business.

Not anymore. The Internet, social networking and globalization changed all that. But the news is bad AND good. Previously a business owner might have been limited in their reach and exposure to a local market only whereas now you can market to people across town, across the country, and around the world. All these people can know about you and your business in an instant. But why choose you or your business when a prospect or market has so many options?

Think of it this way: how many other businesses out there might they go to instead of you? Do you have competitors out there in the business world?

Presuming you have competition (and in reality, who doesn't?), what compels someone to look you up and make the decision to do business with you? Is it the quality of your service? Is your product so much better that the decision becomes a no-brainer? Are you just the most convenient? Are you unique?

YOU ARE UNIQUE! You're unique in an infinite number of ways. Price, service, product or selection are just a few of the ways you can compete.

To be competitive and viable, your goal in business and in your marketplace should be to be compellingly and convincingly different, unique or superior in some fashion.

Do you have any idea why you are or may be better than your competition? You'd be surprised at how many business owners are so busy trying to survive that they actually know nothing (or very little) about the businesses they are competing with or about their own unique advantages for the market.

Let's look at this question the other way round. What if there was no difference between your business and those you are in competition with for the attention, and business, of your target market. What if there were no compelling reasons to entice people to do business with you? If this were the case, then chances are excellent that you would be competing on price alone. This, of course, is the absolute worst thing to compete on because price directly affects your bottom line. If this is the case with your business, then perhaps this is the reason you are struggling and in need of a turnaround plan.

Take a look at this graph as it gives you a good insight into your

And you reduce price by	If your present margin is								
	20%	25%	30%	35%	40%	45%	50%	55%	60%
	To produce the same exact profit, your sales volume must increase by								
2%	11%	9%	7%	6%	5%	5%	4%	4%	3%
4%	25%	19%	15%	13%	11%	10%	9%	8%	7%
6%	43%	32%	25%	21%	18%	15%	14%	12%	11%
8%	67%	47%	36%	30%	25%	22%	19%	17%	15%
10%	100%	67%	50%	40%	33%	29%	25%	22%	20%
12%	150%	92%	67%	52%	43%	36%	32%	28%	25%
14%	233%	127%	88%	67%	54%	45%	39%	34%	30%
16%	400%	178%	114%	84%	67%	55%	47%	41%	36%
18%	900%	257%	150%	106%	82%	67%	56%	49%	43%
20%	-	400%	200%	133%	100%	80%	67%	57%	50%
25%	-	-	500%	250%	167%	125%	100%	83%	71%
30%	-	-	-	600%	300%	200%	150%	120%	100%

Makes you think, doesn't it?

So how do you go about making your mark in your market place? How do you stand up, stand out and make the world take notice and take action to buy?

The first thing you need to be aware of is that most businesses compete on one or more of the following primary elements – price, product or service. Your task is to ensure that you strive for excellence and superiority in one and at least acceptability on the others. Understand too, that people don't buy "things;" they buy a result, a solution, or benefit, and people don't buy "people," they buy beliefs and perceptions.

Rather than simply competing on price, product, or service strive to create a unique "experience" with your marketplace, prospects, and clients. The more unique an "experience" you can create, the more unique the reputation and relationship you can have with your customers. Products and services are easy to duplicate, but unique experiences are difficult to emulate.

What does your market believe about you, your product, or service? What is the perception of your prospects? What is the unique value and experience you bring to or create for your customers and clients?

> "People don't buy "things;" they buy a result, a solution, or benefit, and people don't buy "people," they buy beliefs and perceptions."

Once you are clear on this, you will start getting a clearer picture in your own mind as to the areas where your business can make its mark in the marketplace and where it can increase value and the awareness of that value.

While on the topic of value, what role do you think your employees play in *adding* value? What role do you as the owner or leader play?

While employees of a business may focus on adding value, a business owner or leader must ensure value creation for its clients and market. People today are not just buying a product or service; they're buying a benefit and experience, and perception of the value you delivered in their decision to buy from you – now and in the future.

How has this changed your thoughts about you, your business, your product or service, your relationship to the marketplace, and your competition?

What can you do better, different, or stop doing all together that would make a difference in your business and your selling process?

Okay, now that you are on a roll and before you lose the thread of all these exciting ideas, possibilities and opportunities, it's time to get some of those thoughts down on paper. It's time to materialize some of the excitement going on in your head right now before you lose it.

What you are going to do right now is to write down exactly what you believe are the main benefits or traits that distinguish your business from the rest. What is your pre-eminent advantage — what are you, your company, your product or service great at? Best at? Better than most of your competition? To stimulate and sharply focus your thinking, here are some questions to answer.

1.   What are you or your company great at?

2.   What are you or your company good at?

3.   What are you or your company better at than most of your competitors?

4. What are the primary benefits of doing business with your company?
   - Solutions
   - Wants/Needs
   - Pain/Pleasure

5. What makes doing business with you or your company a unique experience?

6. What measurable data do you have to support your position?

7. What are the weaknesses of your competitors?

8. What should everyone who does business in your industry know that is not widely known, communicated or articulated?

9. What are the common misconceptions about your product, service or industry?

10. How can you best communicate the unique value of your company, product or service to your market, vendors, industry and others?

Your charge and your challenge are to be able to articulate as much value in the most unique, yet understandable way possible. If you can't define and communicate the value and benefits you bring to your marketplace, you can't expect a prospect or even an existing client to fully appreciate you or your company.

Looking Back, Looking Ahead

It's time now to let the dust settle, to take stock of your 10 Day Turnaround journey, and to glance into the future – a future which starts just one day from now. That's right, today is the first day of your new reality!

Vance Havner said, "The vision must be followed by the venture. It is not enough to stare up the steps — we must step up the stairs." If you've made it through the 10 days, you've already begun to see improvements and changes taking place within your business. But your journey doesn't stop here — you must continue to implement the strategies learned here and avoid falling back into old routines and habits.

While you want lots of things to get done, you also want to make sure significant things get done as well.

Once you have your plan laid out and action is being taken, you'll need to move beyond the initial action steps. You'll need to begin moving from the stage of simply surviving your "turnaround" into creating something more sustainable and enduring.

It's usually good to have an evolving plan, a system, or a formula to move simply beyond the urgent to the significant. You'll need to know what resources you need to keep progressing and what resources you have. You need to allocate time, energy, people and capital towards the highest and best use on an ongoing basis. You need to have a system to monitor, measure, and manage your activities and results. You need to have contingency plans and actions poised at the ready if things don't go as planned. These are the ingredients of success and this is how things get done.

Here's a formula for **the best way to get the important – as well as the urgent – things done**:

1. Know where you are and where you want to go. Where are you now, and what would you like to be different?

2. Have a clearly defined vision of the future. When you accomplish your goal or objective, satisfy your desire or need, what does it look like, feel like, etc?

3. Develop an observable, measurable strategy to get from here to there. Does your plan contain specific descriptions of "Who, what, why, how, when and what if..."?

4. Identify, obtain, and align your resources. What/who do you have, what/who do you need? What's in it for them right now and again when you're successful?

5. Measure, monitor and manage your assets, actions, resources and results. What are you/they going to do and how will you/they know if they're on or off track?

6. Plan contingencies — for worse or for better. What will you do if things don't go according to plan - worse than hoped, better than you thought, or simply different than you expected?

7. What's next? After you have accomplished your immediate objectives, what do you want next? Do you want to duplicate it, replicate it, replace it, scale it, sell it, or something else altogether?

DAY 10: Action Checklist

This process can be transformational in moving from your initial turnaround "rough" plan to a concrete plan of action. This same formula can be magical when applied to a concept, an idea, an unfulfilled desire, an unmet need, unrealized opportunity, or looming problem at any stage of your business or your life, now or in the future. I've seen this method change lives at my seminars and I've used this system for over twenty years to create long-term transformations and success in businesses around the world.

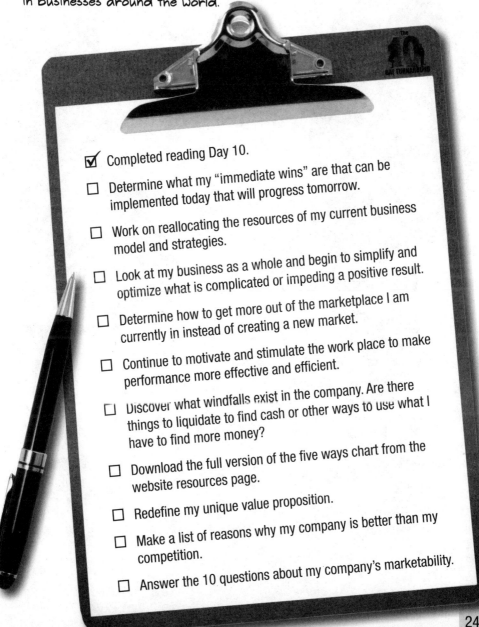

☑ Completed reading Day 10.

☐ Determine what my "immediate wins" are that can be implemented today that will progress tomorrow.

☐ Work on reallocating the resources of my current business model and strategies.

☐ Look at my business as a whole and begin to simplify and optimize what is complicated or impeding a positive result.

☐ Determine how to get more out of the marketplace I am currently in instead of creating a new market.

☐ Continue to motivate and stimulate the work place to make performance more effective and efficient.

☐ Discover what windfalls exist in the company. Are there things to liquidate to find cash or other ways to use what I have to find more money?

☐ Download the full version of the five ways chart from the website resources page.

☐ Redefine my unique value proposition.

☐ Make a list of reasons why my company is better than my competition.

☐ Answer the 10 questions about my company's marketability.

"Congratulations on getting this far - you've done an awesome job!

We're here to help you even more... so read on just a little more."

Conclusion

Final Step

Conclusion
Sharing Your Findings With Your Team

We are now into the application of our 10 Day Turnaround plan. You have covered much ground and I am sure you will have uncovered, discovered or learned amazing things about yourself and your business. Congratulations on making it this far. Now is the time to consolidate all your efforts to realize your dreams for your business and your own future.

The morning following the 10 Day Turnaround is the time to gather your team, share with them your findings, and let them know this isn't just some "flavor of the month" management fad. This is the real deal, the future of the company, the way things will be from now on. Remember that you've made a renewed commitment not to management but to leadership. Your first "defining moment" as a leader in the post-10 Day Turnaround period is to provide leadership by showing your team exactly what you've discerned and what it means to each of them personally and to the company as a whole.

Of course, as you are well aware, simply reading a book and then putting it on the shelf will not give you the success you want or deserve. So make sure that not only have you read this book but that you completed the action steps throughout each and every chapter. Success is not solely an issue of intention – it will always come down to the decisions you make AND the action you take. We hope that not only has this book given clarity to your intentions, but that it has also prompted you to take massive action. We know that the last ten days will have been busy for you and we hope that pace continues into your future. Perhaps not in such a frantic way, but instead with all the actions involved in running a thriving, growing and successful business.

Final Thoughts

It is now 10 days since you started this book and initiated your business turnaround. If, as yet, your business does not look transformed from the outside, you will know from the inside that it is a vastly different place than it was 10 days ago. The extensive questioning and assessing that you have done over the past 10 days means that if it hasn't already started to happen, your business is poised on the brink of massive change.

We congratulate you on your journey. It is not always an easy one — you will have confronted harsh truths and realities about your business, your mindset and yourself as a person as you have gone along. However, the journey has been well worth the effort and sacrifice that you have made.

We imagine that you feel quite excited and inspired to go further. You have kicked off the start of your new business and the sky is the limit! You new vision and goal is starting to materialize before your very eyes and you can take the credit for that. How far you go from here is entirely up to you and your team. Utilize the people around you, your improved mindset, your personal support network and your Mastermind group to shoot for blue sky.

So now rather than putting this book back onto your bookshelf and considering it a done deal, we would like you to look back over the chapters that resonated most with you. Have another consideration about what you can learn from them and, remember, write down your thoughts and plans as they come to you. There is nothing more powerful than visually recording your goals and vision so that you can revisit them regularly.

The www.The10DayTurnaround.com website is your window to taking further action and building on what you have already achieved. Completing this book is not the end but the start of a lifelong journey. You should make it your personal commitment to continue the great work that you have done over the last 10 days and make it even more effective. One way of doing this is to revisit key sections or chapters of this book from time to time in the coming months and even years. And more importantly, log onto the website regularly to check for updates, more detailed information and even greater insights into how you can continue to turnaround your business and take it to greater heights.

Learning from others--and especially the mistakes of others--can compress years of learning into a very short space of time. We hope that you will take the lessons from this book, some learned by us personally and some learned by those we have helped to turnaround their businesses, and make these learnings your own. These people have learned their lessons the hard way, but you don't have to. To follow in the steps of someone who has already gone where you want to go means that you can avoid many of the pot-holes along the way and speed up your path to success.

This is not to say that there won't be obstacles and challenges along the way, but with your new improved mindset you will be ready to meet these challenges head on and turn them into opportunities for further learning and growth – both personally and professionally.

Remember that the key to making a change in your life or your business is YOU! That's right, the buck stops there. If you think you can do it, then you are right, and if you think you can't then you are also right. So be your own best friend, best mentor, best champion and best ally in business. Take everything you've learned and make the change that you know you deserve.

From us to you, CONGRATULATIONS on taking the turnaround journey.

Live with passion, purpose, and profit!

Spike & Darren

PS – We'd love to hear about your success story as a result of reading this book and taking the 10 Day Turnaround journey in your business. If you've got a great tale to tell then please email us at Successes@The10DayTurnaround.com so we can hear all about it.

About the Authors

 If you've been involved in business, marketing or sales for any length of time, you've probably heard of Spike Humer. For 25 years, Spike has been at the forefront of formulating innovative business growth and explosive marketing strategies for entrepreneurs, small businesses, and multi-million dollar organizations.

He's been the "go-to" guy for scores of individuals and business-owners around the world. Thousands of companies, organizations, and people looking for new growth and profitability for their businesses and increases in their personal success have turned to Spike and his advice through his programs, group mentoring, and personal consultations.

As the co founder of the International Achievement Institute his proprietary systems for generating new profits and his results-proven advice have been sought after by success-seeking people in over thirty countries. Spike's been credited with saving some clients from the brink of collapse, while helping others explode their performance to record highs with his wealth of real-world-tested sales enhancement techniques, windfall profit strategies, and performance-enhancing marketing breakthroughs and concepts.

Spike's been a featured speaker at seminars and business acceleration workshops throughout North America, Asia, Australia and Europe. Sharing the stage and program platforms with such luminaries and thought-leaders as Tony Blair, Jay Abraham, Chet Holmes, Stephen M.R. Covey, Seth Godin, Brian Tracy, Mark Victor Hansen, T. Harv Eker, Loral Langemeier, Robert Allen, John Assaraf, Jay Conrad Levinson, Joe Sugarman, Rich Schefren, Darren J. Stephens and many others, Spike has been applauded for his straight-forward, "to-the-heart-of-the-matter" message and advice.

When Jay Abraham (considered by many to be one of the greatest marketing minds ever) went looking for someone to help drive his and his clients' businesses to greater levels of success and profitability, Spike Humer was the guy he turned to.

According to Jay, "Spike is probably the finest business performance enhancement specialist I have ever met and an utter master at finding the underperforming leveraging spots that are keeping your business from soaring!"

Spike's proven business acceleration strategies have helped generate tens of millions of dollars in revenues for his clients and program attendees. He is renowned for creating quantum leaps in profitability and business performance – all in record time.

Spike's "10 Day Turnaround Technologies" have engineered entrepreneurial success stories in a multitude of industries the world over. His "Strategy for Significance" has helped his clients almost instantly earn the attention, trust, and profit-boosting relationships with their prospects and clients. Spike's "Overnight Entrepreneur" methodology has put countless people on the path to financial-freedom and personal prosperity.

As an entrepreneurial advisor, small-business consultant, turnaround expert, author, speaker, and seminar presenter, Spike ranks among the world's greatest thought-leaders and result producing advisors.

www.spikehumer.com

Darren Stephens

Entrepreneur, Author, Internet Marketer, Speaker and Business Consultant

Darren is a self-made multi-millionaire and is a seasoned business executive, entrepreneur, growth strategist, bestselling author and consultant.

Darren was the founder and international chairman of Mars Venus Coaching, one of the world's most respected and leading brands, and is now the managing director of global businesses such as Global Media Corporation and Successful Growth Strategies.
He is also the co founder of The International Achievement Institute.

He is also a board member and International licensing Director of the world's No. 1 eBay education company, Bidding Buzz Global Limited, with offices in 11 countries including Australia, Rome, Paris, Singapore, Hong Kong, UK, and North America.

He's recognized as an expert in the field of business development, sales and marketing, executive mentoring, franchising, international publishing, self-development, and accelerated psychological transformation.

He is the author of 7 best-selling books such as *"Millionaires & Billionaires Secrets Revealed"*, *"Top Franchise CEOs Secrets Revealed"*, *"The Success Principles"* and *"Our Internet Secrets"* just to name a few and he was the marketing genius behind developing the expansion of the *Mars Venus Brand*, now in 150 countries, and the books have been translated into 54 languages and have over a billion dollars in sales.

For more than 20 years, Darren has taught internationally, speaking to and motivating thousands of people in over 27 countries on how to create business, personal and financial success.

Darren's appearances on many television programs, plus articles published in newspapers and magazines nationally and internationally, has made him a sought-after speaker and consultant on the international stage.

Darren has also lectured at University on business management, marketing and psychological transformation. He is a certified Hypnotist, Neuro-Linguistic Programming (NLP) trainer and is qualified in Design Human Engineering and Time Line Therapy.

He is a fellow diplomat of the American Board of Hypnotherapy and a member of the International Franchise Association, Franchise Council of Australia. National Speakers Association and is the founder of the prestigious Entrepreneurs Business School. He lives in Melbourne, Australia, with his wife, Jackie, and their 7 children.

www.DarrenJStephens.com

Recommended
Success Resources

"How To Turn The "Profit Tap" On FULL STREAM & Plug The Leaking Holes In Your Business 10 Days or Less"

Why it's <u>CRITICAL & URGENT</u> to implement a "Turnaround" before it's too late...

It could simply be that, you believe your business is not living up to its true potential. It could also be that you want to understand clearly where your business is at that moment, where you want it to be in the future so that a concise plan of action can be developed to get it there.

<u>Maybe you want to build you business up so you can sell out for a BIG PAY DAY</u> - or maybe you want to take advantage of changes in the marketplace or of a new opportunity, or on completion of your own business-building practice.

The reasons why a business embarks on a turnaround plan are many and varied. However, it would probably be fair to say that during times of turmoil hardship, or a tough economy - **for the vast majority of businesses, embarking on a turnaround plan is most likely so that it can survive.** That is why we look at an extremely short time frame in which to achieve this. It should take you no longer than ten days to come up with a powerfully clear, concise, and actionable plan to transform the business.

To find out more about our Home Study DVD program simply visit our website.

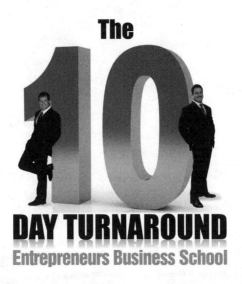

The

10

DAY TURNAROUND
Entrepreneurs Business School

Richard Branson, Warren Buffett, Bill Gates and Oprah Winfrey

These are just a few of the "A-Class" entrepreneurs that have been studied, modelled and profiled by "Business Turnaround Experts" Darren Stephens and Spike Humer, for their book *"Millionaires & Billionaires Secrets Revealed!!! "*

And do you know what the best part is?

Straight off the back from mining and polishing some of the most effective strategies, methods, and mindsets of some of the richest people in the world today, Darren and Spike will be sharing their expertise, experience and knowledge exclusively to lucky individuals in a private 3-day coaching and elite mastermind training experience called the... "10 Day Turnaround Entrepreneurs Business School"...

Meaning, YOU... yes you... can join others and be PERSONALLY (and privately) mentored by Darren and Spike in the luscious and opulent resort setting... and catapult your personal success to levels you have only ever dreamt about before...

Power-packed team who can help you crank-up your personal, professional, and financial success.

Over the course of three short but action-packed days, Darren and Spike will be personally working with you to create a new plan, a new path, and a new pattern of progress for you, your business, and your financial future.

Here's just a sample of what you'll experience:

- The essential elements of becoming a successful entrepreneur

- Discovering your unique purpose and passion

- How to turn your passion into profits

- Unleashing your personal power

- Bridging the gap between potential and performance

- Embracing the mindset of millionaires and billionaires

- Building a brand that will withstand the test of time

- The essential elements of becoming a "thought-leader"

- How to create instant credibility through P.R., Social Media, and interviewing

- How to write a best-selling book

- Modelling excellence in every area of life

- Creating power partnerships through joint ventures and strategic alliances

- Making money on-line, off-line, and everywhere in between

- *And more!*

For a select number of people who are committed to their success, the reward is assured. The question is, will you be one of them?

Visit the website below to decide your fortune, future, and fate

www.The10DayTurnaround.com/ebsevent

How To Write A Book Special Home Study Program:
for Professionals and Non Professionals…

World Publishing Expert & International Bestselling Author Darren Stephens Reveals a Complete, No-Holds-Barred Success System for Getting Your Book to Market.

You will Discover:

- How to have a Best Seller even if you failed English at school.

- How to build a Multi Million dollar business as an Author.

- 21 Simple ways to get free publicity for your new book

- How to turn your hard copy book into an ebook & downloadable audio so you can sell it online for passive income

- How to make $195,000 in just 2 weeks using our book model

- How to make sure you're making the right choice about whether to go with a publisher or self–publish (don't underestimate the importance of this vital decision!)

- The leveraged business model used by major authors to build a multi-million dollar empire around their book.

- Techniques for writing quickly, easily and well even if you're hopeless with grammar and spelling!

- Marketing systems including online and offline marketing strategies

- How to get Major celebrities to endorse your book

- Finding powerful, profitable JV partners to align with who'll do all the work for you.

- How to profit massively from competitive companies weaknesses and gaps.

How To Save Time & Achieve Extraordinary Results …In Less Than 1 Day

What if you could achieve extraordinary results and experience the total satisfaction of knowing just how far you've progressed toward your goals and objectives every step along the way? Imagine the power of knowing you are doing the right things, in the right order, and at the right time!!

The 10 Day Turnaround Priority Management System is a breakthrough in both business and life management that will show you how to align your activities and your laser your focus instead of just simply trying to organize your time, giving you the freedom and peace of mind to pursue your passions.

The 10 Day Turnaround Priority Management System helps you:

- Set priorities using the powerful 80/20 Principle of getting the most from the least
- Break through uncertainty and hesitation to take decisive action now
- Align your actions with your goals and turn them into success and profit
- Set clear direction and plot a course for a more fulfilling role and life
- Create immediate "wins" as well as lasting success

- Regain the certainty that you are in control of your business and life

- Immediately move from an activity orientation to a results focus

- Dramatically increase your level of productivity

- Replace your To-Do list with an effective plan that maximizes your time and guarantees you accomplish key tasks

- Create a powerful sense of purpose, drive and fulfilment every day

- Enhance your project management systems to turn ideas into reality

- Track your progress, learn from past experiences and celebrate your success.

The unique software has been developed from years of real-world success to show you how to gain control over your present and to design the future you desire.

Bringing Essential Knowledge & Book Summaries to High Achievers

The International Achievement Institute is an Global Educational company designed to promote and present world class programs and provide transformative business and personal knowledge to individuals.

To Find out more about the Institutes educational materials & programs like these :

1. Entrepreneurs Business School

2. Entrepreneurs Board Room

3. The 10 Day Turnaround workshops

4. Accelerate Performance Technology Trainings

5. Essential Book Summaries

Change Your Life Today !!

Visit our Website at…
www.TheInternationalAchievementInstitute.com

Joint Venture Deals That Can Make You Millions!

Spike & Darren have developed something of a world famous skill and reputation at understanding how to structure, program and profit-massively by engineering joint ventures, strategic alliances and endorsement deals.

Without exaggerating, it represents the biggest, fastest, most lucrative revenue source, profit centre or income stream YOU could ever create, control and reap financial rewards from.

You'll be able to gain control of products, services, assets, profit centres, brands, entities, markets – for zero capital outlay on your part. In fact, We plan on teaching you 48 separate ways you can prosper from doing J.V. deals... for yourself, for others, or even for us!

Inside You'll Discover:

- Getting the ancillary rights to prominent brands -- on a pure, performance-based payment basis.

- Eight strategic steps to make any JV deal a huge moneymaker!

- How to instantly identify every business's hidden JV possibilities.

- Seven steps to expand your own financial growth possibilities as a JV deal maker.

- Finding powerful, profitable JV partners to align with who'll do all the work for you.

- How to profit massively from competitive companies weaknesses and gaps.

- You'll learn exactly how to make the successful JV deal happen.

- At the very end, I'll give you a 20-step, "mind-expanding," exercise to rapidly propel your deal making career into the financial stratosphere.

- You'll learn seven different ways to get equity/ownership through no-cost JV deals

- You'll learn how to gain"no cost" access to other people's core competencies, skills and expertise

Joint Venture Mastery Collection

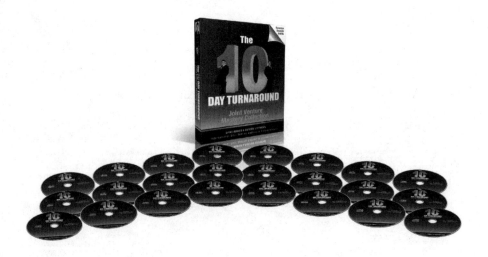

Our Recommend Reading List

- "The Ultimate Sales Machine: Turbo-charge Your Business with Relentless Focus on 12 Key Strategies"
  Chet Holmes

- "Made to Stick: Why Some Ideas Survive and Others Die"
  Chip Heath and Dan Heath

- "The New Rules of Marketing and PR: How to Use Social Media, Blogs, News Releases, Online Video, and Viral Marketing to Reach Buyers Directly" (2nd Edition)
  David Meerman Scott

- "Duct Tape Marketing: The World's Most Practical Small Business Marketing Guide"
  John Jantsch

- "The 22 Immutable Laws of Marketing: Violate Them at Your Own Risk!"
  Al Ries and Jack Trout

- "Drive: The Surprising Truth About What Motivates Us"
  Daniel H. Pink

- "Good to Great: Why Some Companies Make the Leap... and Others Don't"
  Jim Collins

- "Crucial Conversations: Tools for Talking When Stakes are High"
  Kerry Patterson, Joseph Grenny, Ron McMillan, and Al Switzler

- "The 7 Habits of Highly Effective People"
  Stephen R. Covey

- "How To Win Friends and Influence People"
  Dale Carnegie

- "The Tipping Point: How Little Things Can Make a Big Difference"
  Malcolm Gladwell

- "Think and Grow Rich",
  Napoleon Hill

- "Get the Life You Want: The Secrets to Quick and Lasting Life Change with Neuro-Linguistic Programming"
  Richard Bandler

- "Getting Things Done: The Art of Stress-Free Productivity",
  David Allen

- "Switch: How to Change Things When Change Is Hard",
  Chip Heath and Dan Heath

- "Mindset: The New Psychology of Success",
  Carol S. Dweck

- "Rework",
  Jason Fried and David Heinemeier Hansson

- "How to Master the Art of Selling"
  Tom Hopkins

- "Rich Dad Poor Day"
  Rober Kiyosaki

- "Awaken the Giant Within"
  Anthony Robbins

- "Unlimited Power",
  Anthony Robbins

- "The Answer"
  John Assaraf

- "Men are from Mars Women are from Venus"
  Dr. John Gray

- "The E-Myth Revisited"
  Michael E Gerber

- "Test Advertising Methods"
  John Caples

- "The One Minute Manager"
  Spencer Johnson/Kenneth Blanchard

- "Millionaires & Billionaires Secrets Revealed"
  Darren Stephens & Spike Humer

"The real source of wealth and capital in this new era is not material things. It is the human mind, the human spirit, the human imagination and our ability to take massive action and our faith in the future."

Darren J Stephens
International Bestselling Author and Speaker